Is science racist?

Debating Race series

Is science racist?

JONATHAN MARKS

polity

First published in 2017 by Polity Press
Reprinted 2017, 2019, 2020, 2021

Polity Press
65 Bridge Street
Cambridge CB2 1UR, UK

Polity Press
350 Main Street
Malden, MA 02148, USA

ISBN-13: 978-0-7456-8921-0
ISBN-13: 978-0-7456-8922-7(pb)

A catalogue record for this book is available from the British Library.

Library of Congress Cataloging in Publication Control Number:
2016029623

Typeset in 11 on 15 pt Adobe Garamond
by Toppan Best-set Premedia Limited
Printed and bound in the United States by LSC Communications

For further information on Polity, visit our website: politybooks.com

To my parents Richard and Renée,
to my wife Peta,
and to our daughter Abby

CONTENTS

I started writing this book while I was a Templeton Fellow at the Notre Dame Institute for Advanced Study, and probably should have been working on my project, *Tales of the ex-Apes* (University of California Press, 2015). That project came to happy fruition, and now so too has this, and I am very grateful to the John Templeton Foundation and to the Notre Dame Institute for Advanced Study for their stimulation and support.

I have been strongly influenced by the voices of friends and colleagues who have helped me to clarify my own thinking, while sharing theirs. That is a group that includes Troy Duster, Jay Kaufman, Jonathan Kahn, Dorothy Roberts, Duana Fullwiley, Kim Tall-Bear, Alan Goodman, Deborah Bolnick, Susan Reverby, Evelynn Hammonds, Joseph Graves, Richard Cooper, Anne Fausto-Sterling, Pilar Ossorio, Lundy Braun, Terence Keel, and others.

I thank Jonathan Kahn and Julia Feder for their insightful comments on the manuscript, and Karen Strier for long-term wisdom.

ONE

Introduction

Racism pervades many, if not all, aspects of modern society, in different ways. Like other modern institutions, science can sometimes reflect the subtle and not-so-subtle biases of its practitioners. This book is not about the institutions and practices of science, however, but about its content.

I teach two principal subjects as a biological anthropologist: human diversity and human origins. These are about, respectively, who we are and where we come from. For any other society, this would be considered a sacred origin myth, a domain of kinship, by which people establish their orientation in a complex social universe. In our society, it involves the contested scientific domains of race and evolution, both of which are conceptualized rather differently than they were a few decades ago.

Evolution, for example, used to be conceptualized reductively – without bodies, and without species – as simply genotypes and gene pools. Any contemporary discussion of the subject, however, now considers the reactivity and adaptability of the body (plasticity), the reciprocal relations between the environment and the species (niche construction), and nongenetic modes of inheritance (epigenetics and culture).

Race, likewise, has been reconceptualized in the last few decades. Where it was once conceptualized as a fundamental unit of the human species, we now know that the species does not really come partitioned that way. That is a fallacy of primary interest to pedants, like me, and we can call that taxonomic fallacy "racialism." More significant is the recognition that the social and behavioral differences between any two groups of people are far more likely to be due to the processes of history than to those of microevolution. Consequently, the judgment of innate individual properties on the basis of group membership is illegitimate, and we can call that political position "racism."

Nevertheless, when dealing with ancestors and relatives, one never traffics in value-neutral facts. Kinship is invariably bio-cultural. The opposite of evolution – creationism – is so political that its history actually is just a series of court cases in the United States: *Tennessee vs Scopes* (1925), *McLean vs Arkansas* (1982), *Edwards vs. Aguillard* (1987), and *Kitzmiller vs. Dover School District* (2005) are just the most familiar ones. And racism is most familiar as political acts: slavery, segregation, anti-Semitism, once again, to name only the most familiar examples.

This book is about a paradox in science. Both creationism and racism are considered outmoded ideologies. If you espouse creationist ideas in science, you are branded as an ideologue, as a closed-minded pseudoscientist who is unable to adopt a modern perspective, and who consequently has no place in the community of scholars. But if you espouse racist ideas in science, that's not quite so bad. People might look at you a little askance, but as a racist you can coexist in science alongside them, which you couldn't do if you were a creationist. Science is racist when it permits scientists who advance racist ideas to exist and to thrive institutionally.[1]

Consider an op-ed that appeared in the *New York Times* on April 11, 2014, called "Raising a Moral Child," which casually cited "a classic experiment" by "the psychologist J. Philippe Rushton."[2] Sure, why not? He was indeed a respected psychologist at the University of Western Ontario. Herrnstein and Murray's *The Bell Curve*, which notoriously argued in 1994 that IQ is largely genetically determined, sets one's intellectual fate, and differs across large demographic swaths of the American public, cited more than 20 of Rushton's papers. It then went so far as to pre-emptively defend him in an Appendix – rather an unusual step – calling his work "not that of a crackpot or a bigot" (Herrnstein and Murray, 1994: 662). That obviously raises a few questions, such as: Do other scholars regard him as such? Why? Just what does he think his work demonstrates? The answers to these questions became widely known a few years later, when Rushton mass-mailed an abridgement of his own book to the memberships of several professional societies. The unabridged version had been memorably reviewed in the journal *Animal Behaviour* in uncompromising terms: "I don't know which is worse," wrote the reviewer, "Rushton's scientific failings or his blatant racism." Methodologically, the reviewer continued, Rushton cherry-picks data of very dubious quality to make his pseudo-scientific argument, which amounts to "the pious hope that by combining numerous little turds of variously tainted data, one can obtain a valuable result; but in fact, the outcome is merely a larger than average pile of shit" (Barash, 1995: 1133).

Rushton believed, and believed that his data showed, that there are three kinds of people associated with the continents of the Old World (a biogeographic scenario that in fact owes more to the biblical sons of Noah than to modern biology). Moreover, the peoples of Africa had undergone eons of natural selection for high reproductive rate and low intelligence, which he measured via surrogate variables – notably, sex drive, criminality rates, penis size, and brain size; the peoples of Asia had undergone selection for low libido and high intelligence; and the peoples of Europe comprised a happy medium. He believed that the average sub-Saharan African had the IQ of a mentally handicapped European. Yes, he was a racist crackpot. Anybody who ever took the trouble to examine his inane corpus of work could see that.

When Philippe Rushton died in 2012, he had been president of The Pioneer Fund for a decade, a philanthropy that carefully selects its academic beneficiaries, ranging from eugenicists in the 1930s to segregationists in the 1960s, and radical hereditarian psychologists – notably Rushton himself – in the 1980s (Tucker, 2002). Clearly this was a man who was utterly incapable of rendering sober, informed, scientific judgments; simply a wacky ideologue with a PhD and the admiration of some wealthy and powerful misanthropes. Yet somehow he had risen to a position of status and authority in certain areas of science. Indeed, the *New York Times* cited a paper of his in 2014. Sure, the paper wasn't about race per se, but the issue here is Rushton's credibility as a scientist. Every practicing scientist knows that data can be manipulated, and that there is a good faith expectation between the scientist and the community at large. That's why losing your scientific credibility is such a fall from grace: it represents irrevocable descent from a pristine state of full trust and honesty. *We expect you to be able to generate fair conclusions from fair data.* Consequently, to cite Rushton's work is to tarnish your own scholarly credibility, because it says that you have no idea what's going on within the mind or *oeuvre* of the presumptive scholar on whom you are relying.

So, once you know about Philippe Rushton's work and ideas, it becomes difficult to understand why any competent scholar would cite, much less praise, his work. And yet, the journal *Personality and Individual Differences*, published by the academic giant Elsevier, devoted its issue of July 2013 to an admiring memorial of his work. Had Rushton been a creationist instead of a racist, no mainstream scientist or journal would have touched him. Adhering to such a retrogressive ideology would render you effectively friendless in academia. But there was a place for someone who thought he had demonstrated that "Africans" are naturally underendowed intellectually – in academia, in scientific philanthropy, and in ostensibly scientific journals.

Some people feel that psychology is a "soft" science anyway, and that a "real" scientist would easily transcend such nonsense. That brings us to the father of molecular genetics, and Nobel laureate for the discovery of DNA, James Watson. Watson has had a career not just in science, but at its apex, doing his most famous work in his twenties, and winning the Nobel prize for it in his thirties. In addition to two decades on the Harvard faculty, he was the first director of the Human Genome Project, and the long-time director of the Cold Spring Harbor Laboratory of molecular genetics.

And yet he has an odd reputation. Biologist Edward O. Wilson was a long-time colleague at Harvard, and recalled: "Watson, having risen to historic fame at an early age, became the Caligula of biology. He was given license to say anything that came to his mind and expect to be taken seriously ... Few dared call him openly to account" (1994: 219). Watson was always glib in his unofficial role as publicity hound for molecular genetics. Trying to drum up public support for the Human Genome Project in 1989, he was famously quoted in *Time Magazine*: "We used to think our fate was in the stars. Now we know, in large measure, our fate is in our genes" (Jaroff, 1989: 67). Of course, it isn't clear that we have fates at all, much less that they have been identified within our cellular nuclei.

Watson's hereditarian comments raised eyebrows, but a bit later he became freer with racist comments.

In 2000, he told an audience that he thought there was a biochemical link between skin pigmentation and sex drive.[3] That provoked some indignation, but nothing particularly threatening to the reputation of the scientist-pundit. Finally, in 2007, he wrote a book cutely titled *Avoid Boring People*, and explained that: "There is no firm reason to anticipate that the intellectual capacities of peoples geographically separated in their evolution should prove to have evolved identically. Our wanting to reserve equal powers of reason as some universal heritage of humanity will not be enough to make it so" (2007: 326). Promoting the book in the UK, he made things absolutely clear in an interview for the *Sunday Times* (London) that the intelligence of Africans is just not the same as "ours," which leaves him "gloomy about the prospect of Africa" (Hunt-Grubbe, 2007). This time, however, his comments provoked a week-long national furore – hate speech laws being rather more strict in the UK than in the US – which culminated in the cancellation of his speaking tour.

Eventually Watson was prevailed upon to retire from his directorship of the Cold Spring Harbor Laboratory in the wake of the scandal. Yet although there wasn't even anything particularly subtle about his racist musings – that Africans are just dumber than

Europeans – there were still plenty of scientists willing to defend and to support him. My contention is that had Watson been a creationist, that would not have been the case; and that is the theme of this book. I believe that the toleration of racism in science is a problem for science; in large measure because it constructs science as a force of evil, by entering a political discourse and rationalizing the economic and social disparities in the modern world. Indeed, the perseverance of scientific racism can be seen as a bioethical problem, combining the narrowness of scientific education, the arrogance of otherwise bright people, and the misappropriation of the authority of science.

Watson's comments about the relative innate intelligence of races was in fact quite normative for the biology and anthropology of the mid-1800s. Although other scientific fashions have come and gone since then – for example, creationism, the idea that species were zapped into existence independently of one another; or phrenology, the idea that the fine features of the skull revealed the mental traits or personality quirks of its bearer; or eugenics, the idea that the state should take it upon itself to breed a better form of citizen, primarily through programs of mass sterilization – racism has never departed, even though it has taken several guises. Indeed, a testament to the power of racism in science is that it was only minimally affected by the emergence of Darwinism.

Prior to Darwinism, a major question in biology was whether the human races were the products of common descent from a single origin (Adam and Eve, presumably), a position known as monogenism. The alternative supposed that God had created different human groups separately and independently of one another, as different kinds, a position known as polygenism. Unsurprisingly, monogenism had broad appeal with abolitionists, and polygenism found favor among slavers. Nevertheless, there were also intermediate positions. To be against slavery didn't necessarily mean that you believed the different races had equal capacities; it simply meant that you recognized non-white peoples as fundamentally human.

As odd is it may seem today, polygenism actually had its attractions within the intellectual community. Notably, it was unbiblical; consequently, it was attractive to secular radicals who wanted to transcend biblical authority in the modern age. Further, advances in geology and archaeology were consistently showing the world to be very unbiblically old. This made the possibility that God had created other races earlier than Europeans seem all the more likely (Livingstone, 2008).

By the 1840s, the British had outlawed slavery, and the early stirrings of evolution appeared in a very popular anonymous book called *Vestiges of the Natural History of Creation* (1844). Along with the idea that somehow species were related to one another, the author (a publisher named Robert Chambers) proposed that the human races were related to one another as well. His theory was one of recapitulation – he believed that: "Our brain goes through the various stages of a fish's, a reptile's, and a mammifer's brain, and finally becomes human." He didn't stop there, however: "for, after completing the animal transformations, it passes through the characters in which it appears, in the Negro, Malay, American, and Mongolian nations, and finally is Caucasian." And just to be clear: "*The leading characters, in short, of the various races of mankind, are simply representations of particular stages in the development of the highest or Caucasian type.* The Negro exhibits permanently the imperfect brain, projecting lower jaw, and slender bent limbs, of the Caucasian child, some considerable time before the period of its birth. The aboriginal American represents the same child nearer birth. The Mongolian is an arrested infant newly born" (Anonymous, 1844: 306; italics in original).

Vestiges of the Natural History of Creation, while widely discussed, carried little weight in the scholarly community. Nevertheless, it placed the transmutation of species, and the implied kinship of all life, squarely before the public a generation prior to the intellectual revolution triggered by Charles Darwin's *The Origin of Species*, and did, in certain particular ways, influence the thinking of Darwin, Alfred Russel Wallace, and Thomas Huxley.

The Origin of Species, on the other hand, implied a different relationship among the peoples of the world. This was one of common descent, or monogenism, where the common ancestor was no longer Father Adam, but rather, a kind of ape. Darwin's family had been active in the abolition movement in England. Yet even while being against slavery and for common ancestry, neither Darwin nor his friend Thomas Huxley actually believed that blacks and whites were intellectual equals. Huxley wrote in 1865: "It may be quite true that some negroes are better than some white men; but no rational man, cognisant of the facts, believes that the average negro is the equal, still less the superior, of the average white man. And ... it is simply incredible that ... our prognathous relative ... will be able to compete successfully with his bigger-brained and smaller-jawed rival, in a contest which is to be carried on by thoughts and not by bites. The highest places in the hierarchy of civilisation will assuredly not be within the reach of our dusky cousins." For Darwin's part, suffice it to say that the reason his *Origin of Species* (1859) is more readable today than his *Descent of Man* (1871) is that he consciously omitted humans from his earlier book, and thus omitted as well the quaint Victorian cultural prejudices he would later impose upon them.

But the quaint Victorian prejudices of Darwin and Huxley were largely eclipsed by the writings of their German comrade-in-arms, Ernst Haeckel. Darwin and Huxley both greatly admired Haeckel's work; to be sure, he was accomplishing on the continent what they were striving for in England, an acceptance of the naturalistic theory of the common descent of species. Haeckel, however, had broader philosophical ambitions and his discussion of human evolution incurred a debt that his intellectual heirs in evolutionary studies will never be able to pay off in full. Haeckel's theory of evolution stretched from the lowly amoeba to the Prussian military state, but he was faced with the problem of linking humans to the apes in spite of the absence of a fossil record. In his 1868 *Natürliche Schöpfungsgeschichte* (translated as *The History of Creation*), Haeckel made it clear that one did not really need a fossil record to link ape to human, since the connection between his European readers and the apes was present in the non-European races (see Figure 1.1). The grotesque facial caricatures that he used to illustrate the point in the first two German editions of the work never made it into the English translations, but the text itself is clear:

> If one must draw a sharp boundary between other primates and humans, it has to be drawn between the most highly developed and civilized man, on the one hand, and the rudest savages, on the other, and the latter have to be classed with the animals. This is, in fact, the opinion of many travelers, who have long watched the lowest human races in their native countries. Thus, for example, a great English traveler, who lived for a considerable time on the West Coast of Africa, says: "I consider the negro to be a lower species of man, and cannot make up my mind to look upon him as a man and a brother, for the gorilla would then also have to be admitted in to the family." (Haeckel 1868/1892: 492–3)

The point is not to blame the Nazis on Haeckel, as some have tried, but rather to observe how little impact Darwinism actually had upon racism. One could be a creationist and maintain that God created the races separately from one another. Or one could be a pre-Darwinian evolutionist, like the author of *Vestiges of the*

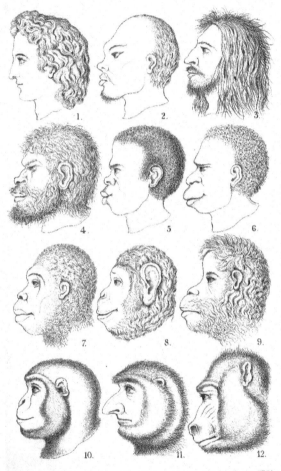

Die Familiengruppe der Katarrhinen (siehe Seite 555).

Figure 1.1 Frontispiece of the 1868 first German edition of Ernst Haeckel's *The History of Creation*. (Courtesy of the Max Planck Institute for the History of Science, Berlin.)

Natural History of Creation, and hold that the races come from a common source, but their non-white expressions represent more primitive forms. Or one could even be a post-Darwinian evolutionist, like Haeckel, and simply see the non-European races as not fully evolved. Darwinism settled the polygenism–monogenism controversy, but still gave plenty of leeway for a belief in the basic natural inequality of races. A book such as Arthur de Gobineau's *Essay on the Inequality of Human Races* was as compatible with creationism when it was initially published in an English translation five years before *The Origin of Species*, as it was with evolutionism, when it was retranslated in the early twentieth century.

Thus, a question like "Were the white and black races created separately?" could be easily transformed into "Did the white and black races evolve differently?" while retaining the significant common bio-political meaning. To understand the British science scene in the mid-nineteenth century involves coming to grips with the bitter arguments about race. The Ethnological Society of London was founded in 1843, largely as a do-gooder group of intellectuals interested in the welfare of indigenous people, and founded on the belief in their fundamental humanity. In 1863, the polygenists stormed away and founded the Anthropological Society of London. Eight years later, the two societies re-merged, using the label "anthropological" but retaining the monogenist – now, Darwinian – origin narrative of the old ethnologicals. In the post-Darwinian scientific world, there could be no denial of the common ancestry of the human races. But it would always be possible to call the full humanity of other peoples into question, even if Adam and Eve were no longer in the picture, with or without Darwinism. After all, the anatomist Georges Cuvier could readily note the points in which he believed that the anatomy of Saartjie Baartman, the so-called "Hottentot Venus," was more apelike than that of a European – but that was decades before *The Origin of Species*.

The branch of science that devoted itself to the physical diversity of the human species, and thus could lay claim to being the scientific arbiter of the full humanity of other peoples, came to be known as physical anthropology. Its early practitioners measured heads in all sorts of standardized ways, hoping – by the doggedly materialistic logic that guided the phrenologists – to learn why some people were the political, social, military, and economic superiors of other people. The phrenologists believed that the brain, being the seat of ideas and personalities, would naturally leave its imprint upon the skull, and one only needed the right scientific methods to extract it. The early physical anthropologists likewise believed that the skull would somehow help them explain European global supremacy. It might be in the size or shape of the head, or the protrusion of the jaws, but such physical markers attested to the advancement of certain races. Other scholars, however, were coming to realize that European global supremacy was actually the result of political and economic forces, not some kind of craniological fate. Eventually, anthropology came to be founded, in the late nineteenth century, on the idea that although lifeways differ and people look different from place to place, there is no causality in that correlation. Different lifeways are the result of "culture," just as different appearances are the result of "nature" – at least to a first approximation. And although there are the occasional points of contact between them, the two domains are generally phenomenologically distinct – different processes working at different rates – and thus human social facts require explanations from the realm of cultural history, not of microevolution.

Indeed, to try to identify the engine of history in people's innate properties is an idea with heavily political implications, as we will see in Chapter 2 – so we do not take it lightly. Suffice it to say, however, that for much of the twentieth century, an argument against the civil rights movement held that black Americans had less raw brainpower, on average, than white Americans, and that this was evident in IQ tests, and that it explained the lower social and economic status of black Americans – which was somehow less significantly a history of colonialism, slavery, and oppression.

Obviously, that is hardly an open question any more, except to a narrow band of ideologues and extremists. After all, we know that IQ is sensitive to all kinds of factors, including racism. Once you learn that Koreans in Japan test far more poorly in Japan (where native Japanese are of higher social status) than in America (where they are of equal status), you begin to see how perverse it is to argue that the average IQ differences between blacks and whites could reasonably be ascribed to innate factors. Further, the idea that intelligence is a one-dimensional, innate brain force has long been superseded. That is not to say that some folks aren't smarter than others, only that smart and dull people are to be found everywhere, and their etiologies are complex. And certainly we now know enough about history and global geopolitics to know that the innate intellectual powers of nations hardly explain anything about their rise and fall (Fish, 2001).

Yet in 2005, the leading science journal in America published two papers purporting to explain the genetic problem with the brains of Africans. Studying a gene called microcephalin, geneticists found that a particular nonfunctional genetic configuration that they called haplotype D was more prevalent outside sub-Saharan Africa than among sub-Saharan Africans. They further claimed to have shown statistically that the gene had undergone strong selection recently (i.e., its prevalence had increased in the population). From this they concluded: "Microcephalin has continued its trend of adaptive evolution beyond the emergence of anatomically modern humans. ... If selection indeed acted on a brain related phenotype, there could be several possibilities, including brain size, cognition, personality, motor control, or susceptibility to neurological and/or psychiatric diseases" (Evans et al., 2005: 1720).

Perhaps that was a bit coy. They clarified their position in their next paper, about a gene called "abnormal spindle-like microcephaly associated protein," or ASPM. Once again, a statistical inference of recent selection, a difference in the frequencies of a recent genetic variant of unclear functional consequence between sub-Saharan Africans and everyone else, and a suggestion that the rough temporal coincidence of the emergence of this allele "with two important events in the cultural evolution of Eurasia – namely, the emergence and spread of domestication from the Middle East ~10,000 years ago and the rapid increase in population associated with the development of cities and written language 5000 to 6000 years ago around the Middle East," may not be a random coincidence (Mekel-Bobrov et al., 2005: 1722). The principal investigator was a geneticist named Bruce Lahn. Still care to give him the benefit of the doubt? He was clearer to the *Wall Street Journal*: "While acknowledging that the evidence doesn't permit a firm conclusion, Dr. Lahn favors the idea that the advantage conferred by the mutations was a bigger and smarter brain. He found ways to suggest that in his papers" (Regalado, 2006).

It need hardly be observed that nearly every aspect of that scientific work has been strongly challenged – from the dating of the alleles, to the statistics that suggested the genes were under selection, to the effect of the genes themselves on non-pathological variation in intelligence. A scientist inscribes crudely primitive convictions about the innate intellectual capabilities of Africans into his research and publishes it in a leading science journal, proposing a precise genetic explanation for those intellectual deficits. And it turns out to be rubbish, like a perpetual motion machine, or wood from Noah's ark. And yet, such racist work can be published in a major scientific forum, while the impossible or the biblical literalist would not have had a chance. There ought to be a simple moral here: we don't want biblical literalists doing science, because they will tend to try to validate their convictions, and thus the quality of their science will be compromised; likewise, we don't want racists doing science, for precisely the same reason.

Now of course, if you believe that science *should* accommodate racism, then you presumably don't worry about the question I pose in the title of this book, and need read no further: science is racist because of people like you, who continue to permit it to be so. This book is for people who don't think that there ought to be a place for racism in science. This is not "political correctness," but the most basic process of science: gate-keeping. Racists should not work on human variation, because history has shown that they don't do it very well, for their presuppositions adversely affect the framing of the research, the collection and analysis of the data, and the interpretation of the results. This is not to say that there aren't other kinds of biases, just that we are already quite familiar with this particular one.

The point of this example is not simply that racist science – in this case, given the intellectual inferiority of Africans, we have discovered a possible genetic explanation for it – can get published in the mainstream media. No, this story has a stranger coda, which shows how deep the problem runs. In 2009, the leading science journal in the world, *Nature*, ran an essay by the same Bruce Lahn, still a respected geneticist at the University of Chicago, called "Let's celebrate human genetic diversity." Defending the (trivial) proposition that human diversity should be studied, Lahn argues: "There is nothing scientifically improbable or morally reprehensible in the position that people, including groups of people, can be genetically diverse. Those who deny or even condemn human diversity adopt a stance that is both factually doubtful and morally precarious" (Lahn and Ebenstein, 2009: 728).

This, of course, misses the point entirely. Plenty of people study, and have studied, human variation; the *American Journal of Physical Anthropology* has been publishing on it for nearly a century. We know a lot about it. Everybody wants the study of human variation to continue. But not by people who bring outmoded racist assumptions to their scientific research. Those are precisely the people whom we *don't* want to be working on this research problem, any more than we would want a creationist to work on the origin of bipedal locomotion in primates. They are ideologically corrupted; nobody should care what they have to say about the subject.

Science historian Sarah Richardson (2011) sees Lahn's work as a redrawing of academic domains and the retention of an inadequate conceptual apparatus for the newly bounded research programs, where what ought to be regarded as multidisciplinary research is effectively co-opted by genomics. "This points," she writes, "to a need for critical discussion among genomicists, and brain and behavior researchers of the relevant disciplines, to clarify the assumptions, aims and ethics of this emerging research" (2011: 430). And perhaps the first question they should discuss is, "Do we tolerate racism?" This particular case, after all, is again not racism with any degree of subtlety; instead, this is "Africans are innately stupider than the rest of the world" racism. There is a false presumption about science, based on nineteenth-century philosophy, that human science is (or can be) free of political value. Not only does history militate against that presumption, but the very nature of the activity makes it impossible. The nineteenth-century view of science was founded on the idea that the scientist (subject) was disconnected from the thing being studied (object), and thus could approach it without compassion, emotion, discrimination, or affection – essentially like a Vulcan[4] or a robot. But the basis of the field of bioethics is that, in the science of humans, we *want* compassionate scientists. We don't want bloodless androids doing the science. That's Nazi science, the antithesis of good human science.

Which raises the second question, and it is a moral-political question as well. Every science has had its own set of ethical issues – chemistry and poison gas; physical anthropology and grave-robbing – but there is one question that only scientists working in human genetics and race have to grapple with. And that is: "What is it about me that the Nazis like so much?"

There is a reasonable line of thought that goes, "If the Nazis like you, you're probably despicable." And that is where the thoughtful scientist starts paying closer attention to the political elements of the research, and starts to wonder with whom they'll be waking up in (political) bed the next morning. After all, if the science is not really separable from the politics, then the politics ought to be scrutinized just as carefully as the statistics. So what does it mean for a scientist to say, "Well, what if racism really is true?" Ought there to be a scientific forum for posing the question, and especially for answering it after it is posed; or should it be taken as seriously as the question, "What if the universe were really zapped into existence six thousand years ago?"?

The question isn't too far-fetched either, since, as I write these words, one of the leading nonfiction best-sellers is a book called *A Troublesome Inheritance* by science journalist Nicholas Wade. Wade's points are that (1) the human species is naturally partitionable into races; (2) the key behavioral features of economic classes and nations are genetically influenced; (3) the major features of history, from the agricultural revolution through industrialism and the Iraq War, are attributable to genetic causes; (4) the Jews are of particular interest as demonstrating all of this; (5) this knowledge is being suppressed by a cabal of Marxist anthropologists; and (6) unlike theirs, his own claims are non-political and scientific.[5]

Suffice it to say that this is obviously very political, so #6 fails immediately. Indeed, since many of Wade's key citations are of conservative political scientists like Samuel Huntington and Francis Fukuyama, and the book's most positive review came from political scientist Charles Murray, co-author of *The Bell Curve*, one would have to be remarkably insensitive not to perceive the politics here. In fact, rightwing extremist bloggers were lauding the book months before publication. Point #5 is paranoid red-baiting, classic in American politics, but not science; the same argument was made by segregationists in the 1960s. Point #4 is odd if the book is ostensibly about race; it seems non-random and relevant that the Jews would be singled out as the only people with their own chapter. Points # 2 and 3 are not science at all, but science fantasy; and point #1 is empirically false, as we will see later on.

Moreover, claims the author, he speaks for Darwinism. That is also false. But we do have a century and a half of people claiming to speak for Darwin in various ways about the meaning of human differences. The earliest Darwinians would casually represent non-Europeans as intermediates between apes and Europeans, sacrificing the full humanity of the non-white peoples on the altar of establishing continuity with the apes. Today, in Darwin's name, come some of the most absurdly outmoded expressions of the relationship between genetics and political history. Darwin is probably turning over in his grave in Westminster Abbey. We can see why Jesus reputedly warned: "For many shall come in my name, saying, I am Christ; and shall deceive many,"[6] and Karl Marx reputedly said, "Je ne suis pas Marxiste."

We can see why racists would want to attach Darwin's name to their theories – it lends them credibility. The point is that we have learned a great deal about human variation; so why are there spokespeople for science who are often still so shamefully uneducated about it?

TWO

How science invented race

There is a lot of confusion over what we mean when we say race is a "construction." Much of the problem involves the fact that in order to rebut scientific racism publicly, we are often obliged to accept the dichotomy of "nature" and "culture" that we now realize to be an oversimplification. But since that dichotomy remains a fixture of popular science, and of public discourse, we often have to say, "No, it's the opposite; it's culture" – when we would really like to say something rather more nuanced. To a first approximation, then, we mean that, unlike a naively regarded fact of nature, which is presumably there to be observed and transparently understood, race is a product of history; and although it is often associated with variation in biological form, it is inherited according to cultural, not biological, rules. And thus, rather than seeing race as a simple product of nature, it is better understood as a product of "nature/culture," the ascription of arbitrary cultural meaning to patterns of human diversity, often in defiance of the biological patterns themselves.

Consider the history of the concept of race. By "race" I mean the idea that the human species comes naturally partitioned into a reasonably small number of reasonably discrete kinds, each with distinct properties. And that, by the way, is empirically false; the human species does not come that way – which may perhaps explain why nobody even imagined that pattern until the seventeenth century. Scholars since antiquity had always described human differences in local terms, not in continental terms. (Some biblical traditions had Noah's sons repopulate the earth after the Deluge, with Ham the father of Africans, Shem the father of Asians, and Japheth the father of Europeans; but of course the ancients had only a limited knowledge of the world, and as brothers, the sons of Noah all looked pretty much alike.)

Although the ancients recognized that people in different places often looked different, they interpreted that variation in local, not continental, terms. The idea that each continent contains largely homogeneous masses, which are different from the masses on other continents, had to wait until the seventeenth century. By the mid-eighteenth century, the idea that the peoples of the world could be collapsed into a few para-continental clusters was being taught by the influential

Swedish naturalist Carl Linnaeus and the influential German philosopher Immanuel Kant.

There was, naturally, some opposition to the idea. The French naturalist Count de Buffon rejected the entire classificatory enterprise of Linnaeus, for whom the subspecies of *Homo sapiens* were simply a lower level than the species of the genus *Homo* (*sapiens* and *troglodytes*, Linnaeus thought incorrectly) and the genera in the Order Primates (*Homo*, *Simia*, *Lemur*, and *Vespertilio*, the bat, he also thought incorrectly). Buffon felt that this pattern – what we would now call a nested hierarchy – had to have been brought about by some process, of which common descent was the most obvious candidate, but which scholars back in the mid-1700s knew to be false. Buffon's insight would later be borne out by Darwin, but Linnaeus's impact on the field of biology in the century before Darwin was vast. The simple reason was that the pattern is real. Animals and plants come in groups-within-groups, as a result of their ancestry.

The impact of Linnaeus upon the scientific study of the human species was that for the next 200 years, in order to study the human species scientifically, you first had to classify it. Interestingly, Linnaeus's classification listed four geographically based subspecies (and color-coded, for your convenience, as red, white, yellow, and black) – but he did not call them races. Buffon, who rejected classification, described human diversity without the classificatory premise, but casually introduced the word "race" into his travelogue descriptions of diverse peoples. A generation later, Buffon's term would be synonymized with Linnaeus's concept, and biologists would seek the structure of the human species in the identification of its core units, the races. Of course, they disagreed quite extensively on what criteria to apply, and consequently on how many units there were, much less what they were – as even Darwin noted in *The Descent of Man*.

The concept of race that was thus produced has two components: discontinuity between groups, and homogeneity within groups. Why did this idea arise when it did – in the seventeenth–eighteenth centuries? It was likely a convergence of four factors. First, long sea voyages became the norm, which tended to strike passengers with the discontinuities of human form, rather than long land voyages, which tended to strike travelers with continuity of human form. Second, the encounter of Europeans with unfamiliar and fluid forms of social organization in other parts of the world was quite different from the centralized and bounded nation-states that they were familiar with; while the economics of slavery encouraged expanding the universe of the potentially enslaveable. Third, a cartographic image became popular at the same time: each of the four different continents allegorically embodied as a woman, later coming to represent the inhabitants of the continents themselves (science, apparently, may well have come to imitate art). And fourth, it was the flowering of science as a method to produce reliable knowledge, which was generally thought to begin with extensive collection and rigorous classification, as Linnaeus embodied.

Linnaeus's own classification of human subspecies was not based merely on naturalistic features like geography and facial appearance, but also on traits like clothing and legal system. White Europeans were governed by law ("*Ritibus*"), yellow Asians by opinion ("*Opinionibus*"), red Americans by custom ("*Consuitudine*"), and black Africans by whim ("*Arbitrio*"). Likewise, white Europeans were characterized by tight-fitting clothes ("*Vestimentis arctis*"), yellow Asians by loose-fitting garments ("*Indumentis laxis*"), red Americans paint themselves with fine red lines ("*Pingit se lineis daedaleis rubris*"), and black Africans anoint themselves with grease ("*Ungit se pingui*"). Clearly, there was a bit more here than mere biology; there were cultural value judgments as well.

But there was also a bigger problem with race, since the term had been introduced without a formal definition. Buffon used it casually, in the sense of a "breed" or "strain"; but when it was combined with Linnaeus's formal subspecies, it became possible to simultaneously have both continents and ethnic groups as categories. Moreover, simply within the continents it was obvious that, say, a Dane and a Sicilian tend to look a bit different from one another. That might imply the existence of even smaller groups-within-groups, below even subspecies (which is as low as scientific taxonomy goes). *The Races of Europe*, published in 1899 by William Z. Ripley, gave an unfamiliar plural for the more familiar singular, and came up with three of them; a revision in 1939 by Carleton Coon identified no fewer than eleven. Fieldwork showed that there was indeed a lot of biological heterogeneity outside Europe as well. Charles Seligman's *Races of Africa* (1930) identified eight of those.

The concept was consequently protean enough to be able to accommodate continental groups like Africans and Asians, physical groups like Pygmies and Nordics, linguistic groups like Bantu and Slavic, and ethnic groups like Jews and Gypsies, simultaneously. Moreover, the descriptive traits associated with each race might not be the products of microevolution, but of history, prejudice, diet, or habits. One such idea was the "racial odor." As Harvard's early twentieth-century race expert, Earnest Hooton, explained it:

I once took occasion to ask a brilliant Japanese student of anthropology whether he detected any odor as a distinguishing feature of Whites. He said that he did most decidedly, and that he found it very unpleasant. Then he went on to say that it particularly assailed his nostrils whenever he entered the Harvard gymnasium. I gave up at once, because I had to admit that his experience coincided with mine. That gymnasium, now happily replaced, was one of the oldest in the country and its entire structure seemed to be permeated by the perspiration of many generations of students. (Hooton, 1946: 541)

But that didn't mean that you couldn't oversell cultural features or prejudices as if they were racial features. The other American expert on race was Aleš Hrdlička of the Smithsonian, and he soberly explained that Negroids were "Not very ambitious; emotions and passions strong but less rational; idealism rather weak;... Love of amusement and sport strong, of exploration weak, of adventure moderate;... Musical ability well represented, but not of high intellectual order; ... Rather careless and free from lasting worries, but ridden by superstitious fears" (1930: 170).

It is hard to know how these ostensibly scientific assessments would have been altered if there were not such a strong correlation between race and economic/

social status in America. The fact that race becomes effectively a social marker makes the assignment of individuals to one or the other category a significant determinant of the course and quality of their lives. The civil rights movement in the US was possible in large measure because of the growing appreciation that "racial" issues and problems lay in the social and political domains, not in the biological.

Race serves to introduce a spurious variable – biology, or nature – into a discussion of economics, politics, and morality. For about 10,000 years, since the origin of large-scale social inequalities, its victims have posed the question, "Why are there large-scale social inequalities?" Why are there haves and have-nots? Why am I not the king, or pharaoh, or tsarina, or empress? One set of answers involves the possibility that the rulers and the ruled are equivalently endowed, and that the social differences between them are the results of long-term historical injustices. The Enlightenment philosopher Jean-Jacques Rousseau famously posed the question of the origin of inequality in 1754, and imaginatively reconstructed social processes – the development of ideas about private property – not biological processes, at the heart of his answer. There are indeed natural inequalities and endowments, but organically, the rich and the poor are, in essence, biologically interchangeable.

A century later, another set of answers crystallized, focused on the assumption that the ruling classes indeed have better ancestries and better endowments than the ruled classes. It had long been common knowledge that Pharaoh is descended from Isis and Osiris and you aren't. That makes the Pharaoh more fit or more deserving; maybe the King is even there by divine right – and thus, the major disparities in the social hierarchy largely immutable, for they are inborn facts of one's birth. But the ancients had only touched on these issues. Aristotle maintained, for example, that some people were slaves by nature, and that poor people were necessary so that the rich could have the free time to be philosophers; but he did not formulate a theory of economic and political hierarchies as innate, immutable, and ordained. That would be the product of Arthur de Gobineau, often called "the father of scientific racism" for his 1853 book, *Essay on the Inequality of the Human Races*.

Gobineau united the blurry idea of civilization with the blurry idea of race, and argued that the European nobility, who were physically coded as "Aryan," were the ultimate racial source of civilizations globally. Civilizations flourished in proportion to the purity of their Aryan rulers, and declined when those classes mixed with the local races. His crucial point was that social inequality was simply a manifestation of an underlying natural hierarchy; Europe needed its hereditary aristocracy because without it, civilization itself would be imperiled. His arguments were reiterated decades later by Houston Stewart Chamberlain in Germany and Madison Grant in America. The important corollary is that social inequality is a fact of nature, and thus not the result of injustice; and consequently nature can be recruited and studied in order to establish just what the innate basis of these social differences is. Over the course of the twentieth century, Gobineau's position has been transformed in various ways, but at root is the political co-opting of science as a means of demonstrating the inherent inequality of different economic classes.

From the opposite end of the political spectrum, other early social theorists, including Karl Marx, argued that social inequality is the result of a history of oppression, and that consequently natural science is irrelevant to understanding class difference. Class difference is the product of political economy, and its solution is simply to work for social justice. Anthropology was founded by a Quaker scholar, Edward Tylor, on the basic premise that the poor, oppressed, and colonized were not inferior orders of beings. Their problems may stem from backwardness, but all people were the same kinds of organisms. "For the present purpose it appears both possible and desirable to eliminate considerations of hereditary varieties or races of man, and to treat mankind as homogeneous in nature, though placed in different grades of civilization" (1871: 6–7).

What was Tylor arguing against? A popular scientific view which held that the non-white peoples of the world were there to be exploited and cheated, if not enslaved and exterminated, for they were actually different grades of people. A leading British geneticist could write: "[A] capable and stalwart race of white men should replace a dark-skinned tribe which can neither utilise its land for the full benefit of mankind, nor contribute its quota to the common stock of human knowledge" (Pearson, 1892: 438). A prominent British paleontologist could write: "It is not priority of occupation, but the power to utilize, which establishes a claim to the land. Hence it is a duty which every race owes to itself, and to the human family as well, to cultivate by every possible means its own strength... [lest it incur] a penalty which Natural Selection, the stern but beneficent tyrant of the organic world, will assuredly exact, and that speedily, to the full" (Sollas, 1911: 591).

So the politics has always been there in the biology; hence Tylor's explicit formulation of a "reformer's science," a science centered on culture, or anthropology – disencumbered from race, or biology, or genetics, which were busily being recruited to rationalize the infliction of evils upon the peoples of the world.

But, of course, that is an assumption. Can we prove that there are no relevant natural distinctions between rich and poor to account for their social differences? If not, then perhaps we ought to keep looking for them. Maybe they will be there, if we just believe hard enough, like extraterrestrial life, or fairies. After all, the fact that we haven't found it yet does not mean that it isn't there. As we sometimes say in science, absence of evidence is not evidence of absence. And it is awfully hard to prove a negative.

Perhaps unsurprisingly, then, given the stakes, every generation has had its ostensibly scientific naturalistic explanation for extreme differences in economic status. Late in the nineteenth century, social workers came to speak of a generalized illness called "feeblemindedness," and in the early twentieth century, the American geneticist Charles Davenport claimed to have found its simple genetic basis. Moreover, he convinced his colleagues of it. Geneticists identified the allele mostly in people not from northern Europe, and in poor people (Chase, 1977).

Other scientists claimed to have identified a natural basis for the social facts of poverty in the size of the skull, or in its shape. Psychologists, such as Lewis

Terman of Stanford, Robert Yerkes of Yale, and Carl Brigham of Princeton, developed and applied standardized tests of intelligence, and interpreted the results as if they had identified a fixed, genetic property to explain class differences. Psychologists Cyril Burt in England and, later, Thomas Bouchard in the US conducted large studies of identical twins separated at birth, and concluded that, for the most part, intelligence and personality are the result of nature, not nurture. And genes for schizophrenia, homosexuality, risk-taking, alcoholism, religiosity, and brain size have all been presumptively identified in the human genome. Granted, these claims have remarkably short shelf-lives.

While all these areas of research may have scientific value, that value does not reside in the demonstration that different groups of people have inherently different intellectual abilities. Those claims have been consistently refuted, but their political appeal is so strong that every generation finds scientists, often ignorant of the history and politics of what they are saying or doing, advancing a racist hypothesis or drawing a spurious racist conclusion as if it had never been done before. In some cases, the data and deductions are actually amusing for what they say about the credulity of scientists when they are committed to a strong bio-political proposition. For a notable example, take the Jim Twins, whose narrative is that they were separated at birth, reunited serendipitously in their late thirties, and discovered that they had married women with the same name (Linda), divorced them, married women again with the same name (Betty), given their sons the same name (James), given their dogs the same name (Toy), driven the same model car (Chevy), and smoked the same brand of cigarette (Salem). Psychologists at the University of Minnesota sought and received initial funding from a private philanthropy called The Pioneer Fund, which we met in Chapter 1, with its long record of bankrolling eugenicists, segregationists, hereditarians, and racists over the decades; and concluded that this, along with the other identical-twins-raised-apart-and-subsequently-united narratives that they had collected, demonstrate the strong influence of DNA upon intelligence, person-ality, and presumably upon the name you give your dog (Wright, 1997; Segal, 2012).

Indeed, the Minnesota Twin Study, the Jim Twins and their wives', sons', and dogs' names, and the deduc-tion of the power of genetics upon one's life course, have been packaged and presented in the "News" section of the pre-eminent journal *Science* three times over the last few decades, and all by the same jour-nalist (Holden, 1980, 1987, 2009). But the question isn't really, "How do you explain these data?" (and, to be fair, the Jim Twins have also been invoked as evidence for psychic connections). The question is, "Why would anybody with any sense at all – much less scientific sense – take such a ridiculous story at face value?" Much less as genetic evidence for anything? Isn't there supposed to be even a modicum of skepticism in science?

Is the source of funding – The Pioneer Fund – relevant to a discussion of the scientific merits of the work? In the bio-political arena, where ideological conflicts of interests are ever-present, of course it is relevant (Sussman, 2014). Ideological commitments constitute the additional variables that complicate the analysis and evaluation of the work, and which most scientists do not have to grapple with, and consequently aren't well prepared to consider and confront.

The field that began the twentieth century as the scientific specialization in the kinds of people that could be found in the world, or as its pre-eminent American expert, Aleš Hrdlička, phrased it in 1908, "the study of the human races and their subdivisions," was physical anthropology. Physical anthropology was founded upon a focus (in retrospect, we might say a fetish) of the skull. Its basis was explained by the early Italian practitioner Giuseppi Sergi (1893: 290): "The skull chiefly furnishes the characters of classification; it shows the external shape of the brain, the most important and the highest organ of man; the skull is the means of the classification of the brain." Of course, you want to study the brain, if you are interested in why people think and act differently from one another, what are you going to study – the pancreas? And since people generally don't let you fondle their brains so readily, you take what you can get – their skulls. Thus, in an unrealistically reductive and material scientific universe, early physical anthropology made a considerable amount of sense.

It was important, however, to distinguish physical anthropology, as science of skulls, from phrenology, a pseudo-science of skulls. Phrenology utilized the same basic argument – personality is located in the brain, the brain is in the skull, and therefore skull form should be indicative of personality – and created personal fortunes on the diagnosis of personal features from the bumps on one's skull (Fabian, 2010). Physical anthropology was different, primarily in that individuals were subsumed by group averages – for the differences among human groups was the central question – and in rejecting, or at least downplaying, the link to individual personality and behavior.

Skulls did vary from peoples to peoples, along with the bodies they came attached to, and it seemed reasonable that a scientific specialty might be devoted to that fact. The earliest scientific experts in the US, Samuel George Morton and Josiah Nott, invoked their scientific expertise in the service of slavery in the 1840s and 1850s. In England, where slavery had long been outlawed, the scholarly community divided acrimoniously over the question of how primordial racial differences were. As we noted in Chapter 1, the dispute between the monogenists and polygenists was rendered moot by the convergence of the American Civil War and the ascent of Darwinism, and in London the Ethnological Society and the Anthropological Society were reconciled in 1871.

In America, the development of physical anthropology was tied to the scientific objectification of Native American peoples. The physical anthropologist was not merely an expert in skulls, but an expert in specifically Indian skulls. As a nation of immigrants, archaeologists in the US were generally certain that they were not digging up their own ancestors, but other people's ancestors. In England, on the other hand, experts in skulls would also be expert in the remote ancestry of their readers. The significance of that role would propel Piltdown Man, the earliest Englishman, to disproportionate significance in paleoanthropology, and would prove particularly embarrassing when Piltdown Man was revealed to be a fraud in 1950.

Although the features of skulls appeared to be quite stable and geographically localized, early empirical studies were undermining those ostensible properties. The fact that some peoples of the New World were known to wrap or tie their children's heads in specific ways that caused them to have strangely shaped heads, which they apparently found aesthetically appealing, suggested that the shape of the skull might be subject to more subtle environmental effects. Moreover, after the French physical anthropologist Armand de Quatrefages suggested (during the Franco-Prussian War) that Germans might not be craniologically true Europeans at all, but invaders related to the Finns, German scientists initiated a racial survey of themselves (Manias, 2009). They found that the relevant racial categories were far less discrete than was popularly assumed; thus, even while reifying the differences between Jews and Germans, they nevertheless found considerable racial or physical overlap between the two groups (Zimmerman, 1999).

By the end of the nineteenth century, many racial theorists clung to the shape of the skull as a racial marker, but empirical students of human biology had their doubts about just how much of skull shape was determined by one's genetic ancestry. The German-American anthropologist Franz Boas used the massive immigration of long-headed Russian Jews and round-headed Sicilians in the early twentieth century to study the effect that life in New York might have on these classically different heads. And indeed, the head shapes of immigrants did seem to deviate from the racial norm and converge toward one another.

Subsequent studies of other immigrant populations, notably of Japanese to Hawaii, confirmed that living conditions had a major impact upon the growth and ultimate form of the body, not just upon the skull. So today, while measuring skulls is descriptively valuable, and skull shape may well be locally specific, it is considered to be a feature of bio-cultural origin, not a fixed genetic feature like the blood type.

Which leads to the next question: What about the blood type?

What Mendelian genetics provided was evidence that some biological things were indeed faithfully and stably transmitted over the generations. And even if they didn't seem to be things like good posture, wit, and a strong work ethic – the features that really mattered to the educated classes – we might be able to use the genetic features available to us as stand-ins, or passive markers, of ancestry, even if not actually the relevant ancestry itself.

The different blood groups were discovered and classified shortly after the turn of the century, and although there was some dispute over how best to represent their inheritance, it was clear that they behaved as a fairly simple genetic system. They managed to group people into four kinds: type A, type B, type AB, and type O. This would have seemed ideal for identifying the genetic human races, but unfortunately the hematologists seemed to find all four blood types nearly everywhere.

World War I afforded the opportunity to study the blood groups of soldiers drawn from disparate populations. Serologists could tabulate the proportions of all four blood types in each population, or they could calculate the underlying proportions of the A, B, and O alleles in the gene pools. Whichever way they analyzed the data, however, they didn't seem to be able to replicate the clusters of human populations generally taken to represent the human races. A critical review in the British journal *Man* concluded that the lack of concordance between race and whatever groupings could be found in the human species hematologically "should be sufficient to convince the most ardent supporters of blood grouping as a criterion of racial type or racial relationship that it may not be of such importance in this sphere as they anticipate" (Young, 1928).

The unfortunate fact was that since the ABO blood group frequencies only really vary within a fairly restricted range, it is not uncommon to find that distantly related populations might randomly come to have identical ABO numbers. Thus, you had people like the Poles and Chinese who had to be placed in the same serological race, but which made no sense in the context of race as commonly or scientifically understood.

The accession of the Nazis in the early 1930s gave some gravity and immediacy to the otherwise sterile academic disputes over the relationship between genetics and race. There had been critiques of racial science before, but the failure of genetics to corroborate those entities posed a strong challenge to traditional ideas about the ostensibly basic natural divisions of the human species. The biologist Julian Huxley and anthropologist Alfred Cort Haddon published a full-length critique of racial ideas in *We Europeans* (1935), and noted that since the human groups signified by the term "race" tended to be culturally designated, rather than naturally bounded, they should be called "ethnic groups" rather than "races." This theme was picked up by Ashley Montagu in *Man's Most Dangerous Myth* (1942).

There was, however, a backlash against the new discoveries in human biology. As President of UNESCO, Julian Huxley commissioned a "Statement on Race" to be a public document for the postwar world. The document, however, infuriated racial scientists of the previous generation, including former Nazi scientists, and they coerced UNESCO into drafting and releasing a second, revised (and diluted) statement the following year. A pamphlet called "The Races of Mankind," which had been solicited and distributed by the United Service Organizations during World War II, was now deemed to be subversive because of its suggestion that blacks and whites had equal intelligence; its co-author, cultural anthropologist Gene Weltfish, was fired by Columbia University for refusing to testify before the House Un-American Activities Committee during the "Red Scare" of 1953 (Teslow, 2014).

In parallel, however, two postwar social forces also began to come into play: the civil rights movement in America, and global decolonization. Here, bio-political issues crystallized: on a landscape of political and economic justice, human rights, and social oppression, biology – that is to say, race – was simply a red herring. To a society in which morons and geniuses are entitled to the same fundamental dignities and opportunities, any patterns of genetic or biological variation are simply irrelevant.

It thus became useful to distinguish between the two related fallacies we named earlier: racialism, the empirically false scientific idea that the human species can be naturally partitioned into a reasonably small number of reasonably distinct groups; and racism, the morally corrupt political idea that natural human groups are differently endowed, are rankable and differently entitled on such a basis, and that consequently individual people ought to be judged on the basis of their membership in such groups, rather than on the basis of their own properties, abilities, achievements, or rights.

While American physical anthropologists and human geneticists struggled vainly to differentiate their presumably benign science from their evil German counterparts, both sciences had to be essentially reinvented after World War II. The new human genetics would be a less "applied" field than its prewar precursor, and would focus on real medical pathologies, like sickle-cell anemia and Tay–Sachs disease, rather than on imaginary social mutations, like feeblemindedness and criminality. Its benefits would be optional, rather than coercive; and its ultimate concerns would be geared toward the family, not the race or nation. Postwar physical anthropology would revise its basic assumptions about its subject matter as well, and focus on the local bio-cultural adaptations and microevolutionary dynamics of human populations. It thus came to a new understanding of the human species "as constituting a widespread network of more-or-less interrelated, ecologically adapted and functional entities," in the words of the Oxford anthropologist Joseph Weiner (1957). The focus would no longer be on imaginary basic sub-divisions of the human species, but on the empirical adaptability of the human mind and body in different times and places. This, in turn, permitted us to differentiate between two related questions, which earlier generations had conflated: "How is variation in the human species constituted?" and "What is race"?

The answer to the first of those questions falsified the idea that race – that is to say, large, natural divisions – comprises a major component of the variation in our species. Clearly, the principal dimension by which we differ from one another is cultural – the adornment, clothing, language, foods, and spiritual beliefs that characterize our everyday activities; and indeed that shapes the science itself. When we – for the sake of argument – ignore the major features of human diversity and focus just upon the biological diversity, we find its primary dimension to be cosmopolitanism, or in genetic terms, polymorphism. That is to say, we find most variation nearly everywhere – the ABO blood group is the rule, not the exception. In 1972 the geneticist Richard Lewontin quantified this result, showing

that well over 80 percent of the detectable genetic variation in the human species was to be found *within*
human groups, rather than *between* them; and this
result has proven robust to all forms of genetic data.
And of the residual variation that is neither cultural nor
polymorphic, the great bulk of that is clinal – that is to
say, varying gradually over geography. And the variation
that remains after accounting for the cultural, the polymorphic, and the clinal is local – those ecological and
bio-culturally constituted populations.

The answer to the second question – What is race?
– became increasingly clear as well, once the simple
answer, "a basic natural division of the human species,"
was dismissed as illusory. Biologists and geneticists
could say what race was not, but it was left to scholars
in the humanities to say what race was. A major review
published in *Science* by the geneticist William Boyd
(1963) actually demonstrated inadvertently how race
was at least as much a feature of culture history as it
was a fact of nature. Boyd claimed to have identified
13 races of humans using the objective and scientific
data of his field. But he had simply imposed his ideas
about human division upon the genetic data of the
human species, and described the results. That is how
he was able to identify five different races of Europeans,
but only one of Africans – certainly not a set of

objective natural facts about the human gene pool. In other words, race was being built up – constructed – simultaneously from the data of nature and from the invisible cultural ideologies that inhere in the collection and interpretation of those data.

Race is thus not the objective observation of difference, but is partly also the highly subjective assessment of how much difference and what kinds of difference are required to place two people in different categories, as opposed to seeing them as simply variations on a single theme. That is to say, the units of the human species are bio-culturally constituted and geographically local. Higher-order clusters of human populations are arbitrary and ephemeral. It is not that races "don't exist" (as one frequently hears), but rather, that they don't exist as categories of nature. The ontological question of race that was empirically challenged in the human sciences in the late twentieth century was not whether or not race exists, but the kind of existence that races have. Human races are bio-cultural compounds, composed from two different sources: the observable biological facts of difference and the cultural cognitive process of classifying. That is how race came to be a unit of anthropology, in the same way that a cell is a unit of biology and a proton is a unit of physics. Moreover, there has never been, and can never be, an ideologically neutral or apolitical study of race. Race is an interesting question to study particularly because it is political – and to suggest that a scientific study of race can somehow shield or immunize itself from culture or politics is itself a highly political dissimulation.

This is, of course, not to say that everyone is identical, or that all groups are identical. That would be ridiculous. They are equal; that is a legal, political status – and as the geneticist Theodosius Dobzhansky (1962) reminded us, identity and equality are not synonyms. At issue is how human differences are patterned – and we now know: first and foremost, culturally; second, as genetically cosmopolitan polymorphisms; third, continuously over space; and fourth, locally. Moreover, given that most human behavioral diversity is cultural boundary work, differentiating ourselves from the other folks by the way we speak, eat, dress, pray, and think, tells us that behavioral variation doesn't map particularly well onto genetic variation. Human behavioral variation is principally between-group variation; human genetic variation is principally within-group variation. Consequently, it seems unlikely that genetic variation could be a significant cause of our behavioral variation.

Another way of thinking about it is to imagine an allele with an absurdly strong effect on personality and behavior – say, a "happy" gene, or an "extrovert" gene, or a "talkative" gene. A German with the "happy" allele may lead a different mental and social life than a German with the alternative "sad" allele. But the genetically "happy" German will have a mental and social life far more similar to that of the "sad" German than to that of a Venezuelan Yanomamo with the "happy" allele. Even if they are both a bit happier, or a bit more extroverted, or a bit more talkative, the genetically concordant German and Yanomamo will have essentially nothing in common.

Cultural processes are what lead ultimately to most human group differences. But those lie within the domain of social history, not neurology or genetics. Consequently, we take biology as effectively a constant, or at least as an irrelevant variable, in explaining the major features of human behavioral diversity evolution. In practice, that means conceptualizing the human brain and body as being developmentally highly flexible, and shaped by the conditions and circumstances of life. Those conditions and circumstances – for the sake of argument, call them "environment" – are far more complex and determinative for a human life than is the "environment" of a fly or mouse, so it is difficult to extrapolate from other species to our own. The human "environment" is not just the sun, air, water, trees, and birds – it is the knowledge of how to communicate, interact with others, make things, and generally survive. There are few things that we can identify reliably as human noncultural instinct, and even those – for example, speaking – are expressed in ways that are strongly determined by the social context in which a specific human develops. That is to say, the fundamental human instinct to speak will develop and express itself differently in Paris, New York, and Hong Kong.

Studies of immigrant communities show that descendants can differ strikingly from their ancestors: economically, behaviorally, mentally, and physically. The most important scientific inference from these kinds of data is epistemological and negative: that the observation of individual excellence or of occupational over- (or under-)representation is a poor and unreliable guide by which to infer a difference in innate potentials among human groups.

THREE

Science, race, and genomics

Assuming that by race we mean large natural divisions of the human species, then the study of human variation is not the same as the study of race because such natural divisions do not exist. One can study human variation, and one can study race, but they are quite different scholarly projects; and recognition of that fact is what brought the science of anthropology into its modern era.

The fundamental unthinking of a central concept is called a "paradigm shift" in the famous phrase of the philosopher of science Thomas Kuhn. In anthropology, this entailed the recognition that human variation could more profitably be described and explained independently of, and separately from, race. Indeed, this disaggregation of race and human variation was the comparable big discovery of the twentieth century in biological anthropology, as our descent from the apes was in the nineteenth.

Race is not a category of nature – that is to say, a formal zoological subdivision of the human species –

but it is nevertheless something very real. We would consequently be mistaken to think that the only reality is "nature." Class differences, after all, are historical and cultural facts, not natural facts. To the extent that class differences may correlate with biological differences, we can see that the reality of race is as a bio-cultural category – the intersection of natural human differences and the cultural classificatory decisions about what kinds and what amounts of differences matter. Those decisions, coupled with institutionalized social inequalities, affect the course of individual lives; indeed, they affect the development of individual bodies – which is why, for example the average life expectancy of a black person in the US is four or five years lower than that of a white person.

Clearly, then, the idea of "race" is rather more complicated than common sense would have it. The fact that "race" isn't there in nature does not mean that it isn't important in people's lives. Many unnatural things are very important, such as money, formal education, prestige, and God.

We ought to be leery, then, of the statement "race doesn't exist" simply because race doesn't exist *as a unit of nature*, or biology, or genetics. For if the only reality we acknowledge is nature, what do we make of political or social or economic inequality? Those are real facts of history and society, rather than facts of nature. Do they suddenly vanish, then? If we synonymize the non-natural with the unreal, then poverty becomes not a problem to be solved, but a phantom to be ignored. And that, of course, is a radical political statement, and a very real one.

We need to interrogate the idea that the only reality is nature, and we begin that by parsing "science." Scientists are trained to carry out science, philosophers are trained to explain what science is, and anthropologists are trained to relate it to the diverse kinds of human social behaviors and thought systems found in our species.

It is notoriously difficult to agree on definitions of big concepts, and often the best you can do is just say what you mean when you use a term. When I use the word "science," I mean *the production of authoritative knowledge in the modern world.* I mean to contrast the activity inherent in "production" with the passivity inherent in the term "discovery" – as if things simply reveal themselves to the suitably primed observer. I mean to contrast "authoritative" with other, less convincing forms of knowledge, such as psychic revelation or textual hermeneutics. I mean to contrast "knowledge" with feelings or intuitions. And I mean to contrast "the modern world" with the forms of knowledge production, however reliable, that have existed in different times and places, that have different basic assumptions about how the universe operates, and consequently how it can be studied. I hope that is clear.

Scientific thought is generally centered on a few assumptions that developed in seventeenth-century Europe. Paramount among them were: (1) naturalism, that there is a perceptible world distinct from the supernatural world, which (despite points of contact) can be studied separately from it; (2) experimentalism, that parts of nature can be isolated and studied in miniature, as it were, under controlled conditions, producing results that can be generalized; (3) rationalism, that reason is the surest path to accurate knowledge; and (4) that accuracy is the single most desirable quality and goal of scientific activity.

Anthropologically, all these assumptions are quite unusual (Marks, 2009). Let us start with the assumption that nature and supernature are distinct domains. A prominent strain of classical and medieval philosophy held that heaven and earth were differently built. Where motion in heaven is circular and eternal, motion on earth is linear and transient. Where earth is corrupt and decaying, heaven is beautiful and eternal. But the intellectual course of the seventeenth century was dominated by the work of Galileo, Spinoza, and Descartes.

Galileo taught that "how the heavens go" was a very different question from "how to go to heaven." Descartes taught that God's reasons for things were inaccessible to science, and consequently we should only focus on matter and motion and the laws that governed them. Spinoza argued that miracles on earth were just events that were misobserved, misunderstood, or misreported. The heavens, or outer space, would become unhitched from heaven, the domain of spirit and miracle, which would in turn become the province of theology, not science. By century's end, Newton had shown that the laws themselves transcended the differences between the heavens and the earth. Things worked the same way in the heavens as they do on earth: Masses attract each other in proportion to the inverse square of the distance separating them; and it doesn't matter where they are. Of course, why they do so, Newton famously refused to speculate upon publicly.

Now, there was indeed something a bit magical about Newton's theory of gravity (it was, after all, an invisible force between things), and we now know that he had extensive interests in biblical hermeneutics and alchemy, but within a few years his work was understood as showing that the perceptible universe was governed by laws and mathematical regularities that transcended miracles. Yet this constraint on the universe is a highly unusual way to think. You know that at the casinos in Atlantic City or Las Vegas the odds favor the house and you're not going to be a big winner, but you still hope, or at least you have fun trying to win. Vulcans don't hope or have fun, but humans do. Every evening, a nontrivial percentage of graduate students in the sciences goes to bed praying that their experiments will work. If we are ill, we take our meds and may also accept the prayers made on our behalf. And need we even invoke the world of sports, where magic, superstition, and prayer coexist with talent, training, and statistics?

The interpenetration of the supernatural or spiritual realm with that of the natural world does not characterize primitive thought; it characterizes human thought.

The value placed on experiment is also quite unusual. Everybody enjoys collecting and interpreting data according to a set of rules – which applies to tea leaves and chicken entrails as well as to nematode embryos. What is quite unusual in the seventeenth century is the standardization of activity, observation, and reporting, so that someone else, somewhere else, can follow the same procedures and get the same result. This involves focusing on the question at hand, so that neither extraneous variables, nor the performer or subject, affect the result. Extraneous variables are dispatched by the development of experimental controls, and experimenter bias is dispatched by the development of standardized procedures and measures.[1] Not only is this inconceivable without the appropriate technologies for precise measurement, but it implies a significant social aspect of knowledge. This knowledge is different from revelation, which is internal, and can only truly be shared by someone who has undergone the same experience. Rather, this knowledge is to be communicated, so it can be replicated; it is accessible to all. It is like the knowledge of a guild, passed on from master to apprentice; and is derived directly from the medieval alchemist's laboratory work.

The goal is objectivity, a term that evokes dispassion, rationality, and truth; the absence of a point of view, no horse in the race, an open mind, and fair and balanced reporting. Of course, we like our journalists, judges, referees, and employers – as well as our scientists – to be objective. In the early 1600s, Francis Bacon saw nascent science as iconoclastic, smashing the idols of bias that arise from the nature of thought, individual prejudice, language, and coercive institutions. On the other hand, life and education produce bias – the only arguably unprejudiced minds might be those of babies, idiots, and machines. And as we noted in Chapter 1, we do want our scientists to grow up to be sensitive and compassionate, and not to be robotic killing machines for the state.

The third unusual attribute of scientific thought is rationalism, the use of logic and reason – a favorite of the eighteenth-century Enlightenment scholars. This is not to disparage logic and reason, which are fine; but any practicing scientist will tell you that inspiration, intuition, and obsession play important roles as well. Unfortunately, since they are fundamentally unpredictable and non-rational, it is difficult to gauge their importance in a scientific, quantitative way. Moreover, it is very easy to impose your own ideas about what is rational upon the universe. Americans famously value efficiency over aesthetics, for example, and used to encode that into intelligence tests, giving credit for the answer that the best path from A to B was the shortest, not the loveliest. Efficiency is rational; admiring the flowers is not. Darwin and Huxley disagreed over whether there were discontinuities or jumps in nature, a question that still divides biologists – and certainly slow, gradual change is more rational than violent upheaval, isn't it?

Just how lawlike nature – especially human nature – may be is actually fairly unclear, aside from our desire to make it seem so. Economists have often modeled human behavior as geared to maximize individual profit, a very rational goal – without appreciating that outside the historical bubble of the modern economy most economic transactions in our species have weighed profit against prestige, good will, and mutual obligation. Maximizing your profits is actually a very weird way to approach an economic exchange (Graeber, 2011). We like to assume that language evolved in the human lineage by facilitating the transfer of useful information; but of course it also facilitated the transfer of useless information, and probably far more of the latter than the former. Nor can we rule out the value of language in communicating about hopeful or possible worlds, which are often fundamentally motivating, if irrational.

And finally, the overarching goal of accuracy is again unusual. Accuracy is not desirable in many contexts; indeed, that may be an adequate description of politeness – a socially acceptable disregard for the truth. Perhaps that is why the image of the socially awkward scientist is such a well-known stereotype.

The point, then, is that science is not a better mode of thought; it is a unique mode of thought that is useful in particular contexts. It has proven useful in getting to the moon and detecting cancer early; and not useful in reducing social injustice and war. Most people, most of the time – even scientists – don't think scientifically about things. They are polite, hopeful, vindictive, imaginative, creative, drunk, awestruck, anorexic, idealistic, sympathetic, enraptured, or just having fun – like everybody else, being irrational and unscientific.

Scientists think like everybody else, and are beset by the same kinds of aspirations, insecurities, and disappointments as everybody else. And while science strives for objectivity, in the realm of bio-political science the best you can hope for is to confront and transcend the biases of your predecessors, while making your own biases as transparent and benign as possible. But if someone tells you that they are unprejudiced and have no bias at all, that's the time to watch your wallet, because you are about to be conned.

The great myth of science is that it is amoral, standing apart from concerns of good and evil, and is only good or evil in its applications. Consequently, it has been subject to public suspicion from its earliest days. Christopher Marlowe's character Doctor Faustus (circa 1600) was the model for the seeker of new knowledge, who is nevertheless subject to the baser human vices of greed, power, arrogance, and lust. Sure, he seeks knowledge for its own sake, but deep down inside he really just fancies a snog with Helen of Troy. Of course he does; who wouldn't? But in the context of the old aphorism that "knowledge is power," presumably we would be most comfortable with high amounts of power in the hands of someone with high amounts of morality. The problem lies in imagining the power that comes with knowledge in the hands of someone who may be just as morally fallible as someone without that power. The person with fallible morals and great power is far more dangerous.

The same insecurity was voiced two centuries later, in Mary Wollstonecraft Shelley's character who is interested in the secret of life, Dr. Victor Frankenstein. He seeks the knowledge of life, but lacks the wisdom to use it safely and benignly, and eventually comes to regret having used it at all. Nearly two more centuries later, Michael Crichton's character John Hammond is perhaps even more insidious, for he is an entrepreneur – with the dubious morals entailed by that identity – and he can simply buy the science and the scientists he needs to help him attain his goal to clone dinosaurs for a "Jurassic Park."

The apprehension – is the scientist part of our moral community? – is a reasonable one, given that the scientist studies nature, and not moral philosophy and civics. If morality is constituted by the knowledge of good and evil and the injunction to do good, yet it is neither part of the scientist's formal training nor revealed in what the scientist studies, then how does the scientist develop into a moral being? Should we not want people with extraordinary knowledge to have at least a familiar sense of morality? After all, we don't really want to train scientists to make weapons of mass destruction for whoever pays them, do we?

A major lesson of the twentieth century is that science serves diverse interests, notably national and economic. Far from being apolitical or disinterested, scientific knowledge increases in spite of a spectrum of interest conflicts. Nationalism is the most visible. The development of poison gas in World War I split the German scientific community, but made Fritz Haber a national hero. The US relaunched Wernher von Braun as a national hero for directing their space program, although he had previously been an SS officer and developed the V-2 rocket during World War II. Satirist Tom Lehrer raised the moral question:

"Once the rockets are up, who cares where they come down?
That's not my department," says Wernher von Braun.
Some have harsh words for this man of renown,
But some think our attitude
Should be one of gratitude,
Like the widows and cripples in old London town
Who owe their large pensions to Wernher von Braun.

Nowadays we rarely bat an eye at the idea of science as a handmaid of nationalism. The state funds science, and it stands to reason that the science it gets will help it, not hurt it. Not only does the state buy physics and chemistry for military uses, but archaeology is often used to create origin narratives for the nation as well. The idea of science as apolitical is undermined by historical and social studies of science, and once we realize that science is political, the question of morality becomes particularly relevant. Christopher Marlowe and Mary Shelley both focused on the scientist as a human being, possessed of the same moral frailties as the rest of us, while nevertheless seeking, and acquiring, great knowledge.

Michael Crichton raised a different moral question for the modern age, when science is a profession, as it was not in earlier times. Today, the knowledge and power that science brings are not only there for the public, or at least the national, interest; they are for sale as commodities for private interest. While most of the science talk about *Jurassic Park* concerned DNA technologies, the underlying assumption that science and scientists are there simply to be purchased often goes unquestioned. We always kind of knew it; after all, the super-villains of SPECTRE never seem to have trouble finding rooms full of scientists to do their bidding (until

James Bond comes along to thwart their plans). What's new is the conscription of biology and genetics into the neoliberal economy, in addition to the chemists, physicists, and engineers. Somehow, there is something a little weirder about the life sciences being for sale.

One of the broadest anthropological generalizations is that, although standards of good and evil may differ by place and time, anyone who believes themselves to be outside the moral realm is behaviorally unpredictable and untrustworthy, and consequently must be regarded with suspicion. While we now recognize that science does not stand aloof and removed from cultural and political interests, there is nevertheless political value in maintaining the fiction that it does.

Consider an undesirable social trait, like stupidity. Now consider that, a bit more than a century ago, the study of heredity was being transformed by the work showing that traits in peas come in binary forms, stably inherited: green/yellow, wrinkled/round, tall/short. It might be reasonable, then, to imagine humans coming in the binary opposites of stupid and smart; and thus did the first generation of American geneticists come to study the transmission and distribution of the allele for "feeblemindedness." Eventually, thousands of Americans came to be involuntarily sterilized for the possession of this imaginary gene.

A parallel case could be made for homosexuality, if we imagine dichotomous states governed by a single stably inherited genetic factor, and one's sexual classification fated by the facts of conception. In that case, as the Nazis appreciated, to eliminate the undesired condition, you eliminate the people with the condition. After World War II, it became scientifically fashionable to reject the imaginary dichotomous genetics, while nevertheless still accepting the dichotomous thought that held genes in opposition to learning, and heterosexuality in opposition to homosexuality. If homosexuality were now considered to be developed or acquired, then eliminating the people would never eliminate the condition, for it would always be acquirable; hence an argument for greater tolerance for homosexuality. The "learned behavior" argument, however, was a two-edged sword, in that it raised the shadow of children being "taught" homosexuality. By the 1990s, the pendulum was swinging back toward the argument that "you can't learn homosexuality; it's innate," based on facile interpretations of twin data, brain data, and DNA data. Of course, the accurate answer – that we really don't understand the etiology of human sexuality, and that certainly it is more complicated than homo-versus-hetero and genetic-versus-learned – is less politically useful than either of the simpler answers (Lancaster, 2003). The famous (if false) 1993 "homosexuality gene" on chromosome X, region q28, was embraced by the gay community for presumably establishing that sexual preference is innate, and a fact of nature; when, like race, sex is a fact of bio-politics.

In the new millennium, however, genetics has become more than just a scientific authority for political positions; it has also become a scientific cash cow. Indeed, the principal difference between the genetics of a generation ago and today's genomics has been that DNA – the focus of genomics – can be commodified and sold. Whether composing a narrative of personal ancestry, tying a criminal to a crime scene, testing for a disease predisposition, or seeing that your child has a gene that might make them a better sprinter, genetic information is a marketable commodity, which means that the line between science news features and biotech infomercial has become considerably blurrier than it used to be.

Biotechnology has existed for decades, but the modern era of biology and business can usefully be marked by a dinner in 1998 in which James Watson, Nobel Laureate and head of the Human Genome Project, touted some cancer research by a friend of his hyperbolically to a reporter for the *New York Times*. Watson's prediction that this work would cure cancer within a few years made it to the front page, and led to a precipitous rise in the stock price of the company that made the pharmaceutical being tested by the colleague. The work, of course, did not cure cancer, but it did show how readily fortunes could be made with some favorable publicity for a hopeful research angle (Marshall, 1998). But since most hopeful research angles don't pan out, it's essentially promoting an investment in science fiction, with the slight erasure of the distinction between science fiction and science.

This was probably the first recognition that genomics and neoliberal capitalism could be bedfellows, regardless of the truth value of the scientific claims being made. Much genomic information today comes from corporate sources, where the goal of the advancement of knowledge is accompanied by the goal of profits. Consequently, one is now obliged to ask "Cui bono?" (who benefits?) when evaluating genetic claims. The claim, for example, that "obesity is genetic" would stand to benefit the fast-food industry (obesity is genetic, so have another Big Mac), and stand to harm the diet and fitness industries (obesity is genetic, so why bother dieting?). Once again, the complex reality is of no interest to either side.

The most unexpected aspect of the emergence of genomic science in the twenty-first century is the commercialization of ancestry that has accompanied it, profitably reifying not just race, but all kinds of ancient and modern identities. The issue here will be parallel to the conflict of interests that was identified by Jesus in the Sermon on the Mount. Jesus says that you cannot serve both God and money, for it gives you two masters, an obvious conflict of interests for those who aspire to holiness. But can you serve both Genomics and money? If you aspire to true knowledge, can you avoid having it corrupted by that bag of money on the table?

Probably not, and for the same reason; when science compromises with truth, its cultural authority quickly erodes.

The new field is known as recreational genomic ancestry testing, and it markets genomic data – science – along with fabricating meaning for the data. There are three types of tests, rooted in matching one DNA sample (usually yours) to a database: mitochondrial DNA (mtDNA), which we inherit clonally from our mothers; Y-DNA, which men inherit from their fathers; and autosomal DNA, which is a unique mixture of both of our parents. Each test gives you different sorts of information – mtDNA, for example, is inherited from only one ancestor in every generation (your mother's mother's...mother), thus rendering 15 of your 16 great-great-grandparents invisible to this test. Just like 127 of your 128 great-great-great-great-great-grandparents. So it isn't really your ancestry; it's a sort of marker of a small bit of your ancestry, and the further back in time you go, the smaller a bit of your ancestry it actually is – retreat only a few centuries and your mitochondrial ancestor has effectively been infinitely diluted out, and her significance is merely genetic homeopathy.

But your autosomal DNA is what we mean by "your genome" and it represents a mash-up of all 128 of those great-great-great-great-great-grandparents. Now, that's a lot of great-great-great-great-great-grandparents, and that's just seven generations ago. There are of course, some things that can be said about you, with varying degrees of reliability, from your DNA. The trick is to know which things are more reliable. There are, after all, companies claiming to be able to tell you that you have the Y-chromosome of Moses – which might be true, if the biblical book of Exodus is more or less true and there really was a lawgiver named Moses, who had a brother named Aaron, who founded the priestly lineage, and if the Y-chromosome form found most commonly among Jews who claim to be priests now represents the one descended from Aaron, which has been passed on faithfully from father to son along with the priesthood for thousands of years.

What might be true, however, is again science fiction. What is most likely true is science. That gets to the crucial lesson here: the technology has produced the ability to tell a story around a set of data. Many stories, in fact, but one in particular is for sale. It's about you, and your ancestors (Lee et al., 2009). It is a story consistent with the data, so it might well be true; if it's not true, nobody is hurt – and people will pay for it. Some stories involve linking you up to a famous ancestor, or linking African Americans to putative ancestral tribes in Africa (Nelson, 2016). Some link Europeans to their ancestral "mitochondrial clans" in the Pleistocene; others break down your ancestry into racial percentages; and still others promise to naturalize the boundaries around ethnic groups whose membership is political and may be contested (Nash, 2008; Abu el-Haj, 2012; TallBear, 2013).

What is significant about this work is not its accuracy, but its marketability, and consequently it occasionally pits academic geneticists against entrepreneurial geneticists. One prominent geneticist complains that the stories entrepreneurs tell often come from "cherry-picking" the data (Jobling, 2012); another refers to some marketed claims as "genetic astrology" (Thomas, 2013). And after sequencing your DNA, some companies go on to enter you into their database, which they then sell to pharmaceutical or biomedical companies. *You paid to become their data.*

Clearly there is scientific value in comparing DNA sequences to answer specific questions about the identification of criminals, or the cause of genetic disease, or one's immediate parentage. But DNA is not so good with the more general question, "Where did I come from?" Or at least no better than a good look in the mirror.

Let us say, for the sake of argument, that you claimed to be a direct descendant of George Washington, or anyone else comparably admirable, who lived, say ten generations ago. The biological question is, "How much of your DNA did you inherit from him?" That question can be answered by knowing how many other lineal ancestors you have ten generations ago. One generation ago, you had two parents, each of whom had two parents, and so on. Ten generations ago, you had 2^{10} ancestors, or more than 1,000 lineal progenitors. While that number is an upper limit, assuming you are perfectly outbred, it nevertheless indicates that whatever DNA you may have inherited from George Washington is at best a minuscule proportion of your genome. Moreover, it is also a miniscule proportion of George Washington's genome, and consequently the chance that what you happened to inherit actually represents George Washington's best DNA is quite small. Clearly, then, being George Washington's lineal descendant is biologically meaningless; the meaning lies in the realm of the imaginary – the social, political, and ideological capital that having a prominent ancestor represents. Indeed, the symbolic power of the ancestor often rises in proportion to the remoteness of the ancestry, as the biological significance recedes toward zero.

Consider the premise of *The Da Vinci Code*, that there might be people alive today who are descendants of Jesus. But biologically speaking, how many other people would they also be the descendants of? If we assume 25 years per generation, Jesus would have lived about 80 generations ago. And 2^{80} ancestors in 30 AD works out to about a septillion (a number with 24 zeroes behind it) ancestors in that generation along with Jesus.

But what a strange calculation – that anyone would have more ancestors than people alive at the time – in this case, by many orders of magnitude. This paradox is known as pedigree collapse,[2] and it reveals the bio-cultural aspect of ancestry, retaining symbolic meaning in the face of effectively infinite genetic dilution, much as devotees of homeopathic medicines believe about their elixirs.

Of course, you could have received a tiny chunk of DNA from that first-century ancestor, because that is what ancestry is, biologically – the transmission of

DNA. But here is the kicker: any ancestor in your bloodline that far back is probably also in mine. Think about it. There are a septillion slots to fill in your first-century pedigree, and perhaps a few tens of millions of people alive back then to fill them. Anyone alive back then, who has anything represented in today's human gene pool, is as likely to be among my septillion ancestors as to be among your septillion ancestors. There may be quantitative variation in our pedigrees – he may recur more times in my pedigree than in yours – but there isn't mathematical room for there to be qualitative variation. There simply weren't enough people alive, and everybody's got to have two parents. We are all biological relatives, we are all inbred, and the farther back we go, the less meaning biological differences have, because for every generation that we retreat, the number of our ancestors doubles, yet the size of the human species diminishes. Each of us has a septillion ancestors being drawn from a much smaller pool of people who lived 80 generations ago.

And that is only a couple of thousand years ago. Demographic modelers have shown that one only has to go back as far as the Neolithic, 10,000 years ago, to be mathematically fairly certain that everyone alive today is drawn from the same pool of ancestors. That is, of the people on earth 10,000 years ago, any particular person was the ancestor of nobody alive today or of everybody alive today; nobody back then was the ancestor of only some people alive today (Rohde et al., 2004).[3] For modern people, ancestry that far back in time differs only quantitatively, not qualitatively.

So if individual variation in biological ancestry is effectively meaningless by 10,000 years ago, it is even more meaningless 20,000 years ago. And we are now in a position to understand the significance of your mitochondrial clan mother, which can be revealed to you for £199 by the respectable genetic genealogy service called oxfordancestors.com. As the company's founder, Professor Bryan Sykes, notes in his book, *The Seven Daughters of Eve*, when the computer is asked to find patterns in the similarities of European mitochondrial DNAs, it divides them into seven primary clusters, and Sykes gives them each mythologized names and identities. And it sounds cool, so you pay your money to "discover to which of the clans you belong, and from which ancestral mother you are descended." And you learn that your mtDNA sorts you into "the clan of Xenia," which was "founded 25,000 years ago."[4]

Now, of course, there is no "clan of Xenia." That is entirely metaphorical. Members of a real clan stand in a particular and recognized social relationship to one another. The members of the "clan of Xenia" are united by no one other than the geneticist.[5] Since mtDNA is inherited from one's mother, back when the tree of similarity of the modern mtDNAs coalesces into a single founder sequence, that founder must have been a woman. And with a knowledge of the mutation rate, you can calculate that the mtDNA founder sequence arose 25,000 years ago. So it's a woman, we might as well call her Xenia, and you've inherited her DNA and so you are her descendant.

But so am I. Because of pedigree collapse, if Xenia from 25,000 years ago is your ancestor, she is mathematically constrained to be mine as well. And even though she left you her mitochondrial DNA, there's no telling what chromosomal DNA she passed on to me; it might even be more than the mitochondrial DNA she passed on to you!

Once you realize that "Xenia" is my ancestor too, although not my mitochondrial ancestor, you might feel as though this is some kind of game. It's all legitimate, honest, and ethical, but it is business, and business is about product, marketing, and sales. The game is not in the science, which is real high-tech DNA sequence data, but in the fabrication of meaning for those data. What is for sale is neither science nor facts of nature, but a contrived feeling of connection to others, and to a mythic history.

Ultimately, population genetic data simply lend themselves quite readily to reification, in which a statistical population becomes confused with a natural population. It is not terribly difficult to find studies that generalize about "Africans" from the genetic analysis of 100 central African pygmies, or a few dozen Ibos from Nigeria, or African Americans. We might think of that as "top-down" reification. Conversely, while any two populations can be genetically analyzed and contrasted – say, Hopis and Navajos, or French and Germans, or Xhosa and Zulu, the nature and extent of those differences never tell us that those gene pools are at all distinct from one another, or that Hopis, Navajos, French, Germans, Xhosa, and Zulu are in any sense "natural" categories. We might think of that as "bottom-up" reification.

In the study of human prehistory, the urge to reify populations long preceded the introduction of genomics into the mix. Paleontologist George Gaylord Simpson, surveying the entire Class Mammalia, lamented the biopolitics of human classification as early as 1945: "Perhaps it would be better for the zoological taxonomist to set apart the family Hominidae and to exclude its nomenclature and classification from his studies" (p. 188).

After all, any discussion of the taxonomic status of Neanderthals (species *Homo neanderthalensis* or subspecies *Homo sapiens neanderthalensis*?) must also collide with the pseudo-taxonomic status of Africans, Irish, Jews, Hispanics, Sami, and other human group identities. That certainly is not the case for discussions of the taxonomic status of *Drosophila melanogaster*, the fruit fly; or *Microtus ochrogaster*, the prairie vole.

But even Simpson's cynicism would not have prepared him for the Denisovans – a race of semi-people named for the cave in Siberia in which a 50,000-year-old finger bone was found, and DNA successfully extracted from it. The mitochondrial DNA suggested it to be different from both Neanderthal and human; nuclear DNA suggested it to be a divergent Neanderthal female. And the geneticists produced trees and maps charting the evolution and migration of "the Denisovans." Whatever its bearer was, the analysts of the finger bone made the journey from real genome to imaginary population with breathtaking speed. That's not to say that the bearer of the finger bone was an orphan, cut off from others of her kind – simply that we have no idea what, or who, or even when or where her "kind" actually was. Much less whether the category "human" contrasts with, or embraces, her.

However, if you are interested to know how much of the Denisovans is in your genome, there are companies that will gladly tell you, for a price.

FOUR

Racism and biomedical science

If race is not a natural division of the human species, then what is it? Race is a shorthand, one of many that people employ for knowing something about someone without actually knowing it at first hand. In this case, it tells us that since people fall into a small number of natural groups, they each have the properties of those groups.

The fallacy that a person is the embodiment of their ancestry, or continent, or nation is a fallacy of essentialism, and in the context of unequal political and economic status and rights, we recognize this as a moral evil. But the fallacy it presupposes – that there are a few natural kinds of people in the first place – is a taxonomic fallacy, and is not so much a moral evil as an empirical falsehood. Since the Enlightenment, it had been a scientific practice to classify things formally. Linnaeus did it for all species, including humans. But Linnaeus only assigned a few domestic animals, and us, to have formal subspecies below the species. And, as we noted in Chapter 2, Linnaeus assigned each of these human subspecies a color, and general properties about their personalities, legal systems, and clothing.

In this case, the shorthand tells you that if you know someone's color, you can make a good guess as to their clothing; because there is some intimate connection between the features in question, and the natural divisions of the species. Linnaeus, we can now see, was interpreting the human species in the context of the medical knowledge of his day, which still saw the body as composed of a balance of humors: blood (*sanguis*), phlegm, yellow bile (*chole*) and black bile (*melanchole*). And sure enough, Linnaeus scored the European, African, American, and Asian personalities as *sanguineus* (hearty), *phlegmaticus* (lazy), *cholericus* (irritable), and *melancholicus* (sad), respectively.

This shorthand is a set of narratives that help us answer the question, "Who am I?" Humans generally answer that question relationally: the daughter of someone, the sister of someone, the aunt of someone, the teacher of someone, the friend of someone, the partner of someone, the employee of someone – that is who you are. You learn who you are by situating yourself in connection to others. And the others are not products of nature, either. The most fundamental narrative of identity divides people into relatives and nonrelatives, in defiance of biology, since we are all related, to greater or lesser degrees. We create a qualitative break where none exists in nature, and we make that distinction between relatives and non-relatives in locally specific ways.

This was the first discovery of modern anthropology: that something as seemingly natural as "relatedness" could in fact be regularly tweaked, manipulated, or flat-out contradicted, while maintaining perfect functionality. Different peoples think of relatives differently, structure their lives accordingly, and yet survive. In so doing, they come to understand who they are by learning how they fit in. And of course they do so in locally specific ways.

More generally, our narratives of identity are made by first understanding the kinds of people that there are (relatives and non-relatives, brothers, daughters, and other statuses) and learning that this is what you are. These are the kinds of people there are, and you are that kind – at least in a particular context. For Linnaeus, continents contain discrete and homogeneous kinds of people. This of course integrates a great deal of cultural information into the ostensibly natural subspecies divisions. And this is fundamentally different knowledge than a fruit fly has to work with.

Are you Labour, Conservative, Republican, Democrat, or Independent? Are you gay, straight, or bi? Do you root for Manchester United or Liverpool? Yankees or Red Sox? You can be over 21 or under 21. Which are you? Catholic, Protestant, Jewish, Hindu, or Muslim? Hispanic or non-Hispanic? Indian or non-Indian? College graduate or not? What part of the country are you from?

Significantly, none of those questions that help establish a British or American identity rests easily on a distinction of nature or biology. Even the question about your age is a political binary, but a biological continuum; and it is not even a reliable biological marker, since, at 21, some people will have had their wisdom teeth erupt, and others won't have. But regardless of their maturity by dental eruption, they can all legally have a beer in both nations. The mistake lies in thinking that the ability to classify people into meaningful categories implies that those categories are units of nature. The answer to the question "Who am I?" is found in the domain of the non-material, non-biological, and non-natural – in the symbolic, social, and relational worlds that are always volatile to some extent, but which were largely made by our ancestors, so we could slot ourselves in.

You can see this at work in the other great narrative we humans tell, namely: "Where did I come from?" In biblical times, these two questions were often intertwined: the ancient Hebrews not only considered themselves to be Hebrews, but descended from an ancient ancestor (somewhere in between Noah and Abraham) called Heber. They considered the Egyptians not only to be a people called Mizraim, but to be descended from someone named Mizraim. The question of their identity and the question of their origin had the same answer.

In science, our answers to the question of where we came from are stories that center around a descent from the apes. And once again, our units are not units of nature, but units of narrative, whose elements are already there for us: the human lineage is composed of species, just like the units of paleontology and ecology. Back in 1945, paleontologist George Gaylord Simpson was reviewing the literature on mammal evolution, but when he got to humans, he found it impenetrable, as we noted in Chapter 3. He had an idea why it was so impenetrable to him, as well: "A major reason for this confusion is that much of the work on primates has been done by students who had no experience in taxonomy and who were completely incompetent to enter this field, however competent they may have been in other respects" (Simpson 1945:181).

Granted that many of the workers in the field may have been trained principally in medical anatomy rather than in evolutionary paleontology, Simpson thought it was reasonable to expect that an expert on the species of other kinds of mammals should be able to translate freely to the literature on human evolution, because the units ought to be the same. But he misunderstood the species in our own lineage, for these taxonomic entities are not like the taxa of biology. Simpson hoped to study his ancestors dispassionately and rationally, as perhaps Vulcans contemplate their ancestors. But a logical, Vulcan approach to ancestry involves not dividing people into relatives and non-relatives, for they acknowledge that, rationally and logically, everyone is related. They also do not consider ancestry beyond the twelfth generation (approximately 300 earth-years, because in the twelfth generation, every organism had 4,096 ancestors, which is rather a lot to track); and each contributed less than one-fortieth of one percent of your genome, so none of them is particularly genetically significant. But we aren't Vulcans, we are Earthlings, and we treat our kinship and descent in all kinds of meaningfully irrational ways, even in science. In fact, that was probably the first major discovery made by anthropology: That *nobody* conceptualizes their descent and relatedness in a purely rational and objective way.

There is much we would like to know of our ancestors, which they cannot tell us. For example, we can talk about Neanderthals, but we cannot really tell whether the category "human" ought to incorporate them, or contrast against them. This is participation in the construction of an authoritative narrative of our ancestry. The units here, the species, are not comparable to the species the zoologist is familiar with, for these are not units of ecology, but units of story.[1]

This is not to say that they don't overlap, and that there were no zoological species in our ancestry. The problem is that whatever those zoological units were are now inaccessible to us, and so we can tell quite different origin stories from the same empirical database (Landau, 1991). Moreover there are all kinds of diverse pressures – nationalist, ideological, financial, egotistical – also going into the construction of those origin stories. This is, consequently, only partly an empirical exercise, but also significantly a hermeneutic exercise.

The familiar Neanderthals, the unfamiliar Denisovans, the new *Homo naledi*, and the old *Homo erectus* are all elements of our origin story, part of the bricolage of origin story-making.[2] There is consequently no true or false answer to *Homo naledi* or *Homo neanderthalensis* as a zoological species; for the category of zoological species does not apply to things like them. To the extent that our ancestry is populated by species, those species are attempts to impose a taxonomic structure, which we assume ought to be there, upon an assortment of fossils from various times and places, with diverse anatomies, representing distinct lineages different from one another and yet connected in complex ways. There are a lot of ways of doing it, and they are all sensitive to the conditions under which the science itself is practiced. Indeed, the famous Darwinian metaphor of divergent twigs of a tree-branch is probably inappropriate here: human prehistory is probably more like a capillary system, a railroad trellis, a rhizome, or a river delta (Ackermann et al., 2016).

Such is the longstanding taxonomic fallacy in grappling with the science of who we are and where we come from. On a bio-political terrain, it is not familiar biological taxonomy, however much it may seem to be. The scientific story of the human tree has always been full of pseudo-taxa, disconnected from whatever biology may be there.

If the Neanderthals and the Denisovans are not like zoological species, then what might they be like? Zoologically, they could only be subspecies, as Linnaeus indeed considered unfamiliar peoples to be. In other words, the classification of extinct humans intergrades into the classification of extant humans. This fallacy – imposing taxonomic structure upon our ancestry, and mistaking the bio-political categories of our story for natural units – is the same fallacy we find at the heart of race. For race, the meaningful story is "Who are we?" rather than "Where did we come from?" but the problem is the same, mistaking bio-political units of people for zoological units of people. And those two questions are invariably intertwined, whether the answer comes from science or from any other system of explanatory narrative.

The names we give to groups of people do not demarcate categories of nature that are recognizable and familiar to the zoologist. One of the primary discoveries of twentieth-century social science is that race (being named groups) and human diversity (being patterns of difference) are two very different things. Race is a process of classification, whose categories are far more distinct than human variation is. Race is discrete and homogeneous; human diversity is anything but. Race is a set of narratives about the structure of the human species; human diversity is empirically discordant from those narratives. The way to understand race is humanistically, for it is the product of history and politics, and is experienced; the way to understand human diversity is scientifically, for it is the result of bio-cultural naturalistic processes, and can be measured and analyzed.

There is nothing in biology – except that it presents a symbolic marker of other things – to signify fear of

Muslims or vaguely Middle Eastern-looking people generally. Muslim extremists can inspire fear and terror today, much as anarchists did a century ago, detonating bombs in public spaces in big cities – except that in the US back then, the political issues were somewhat different, the suspect ethnicity was Italian, and the suspect religion was Catholic. Waves of anti-immigration sentiments follow waves of impoverished immigrants into western Europe, much as they did into America a century ago. And then, as now, while the immigrants may be distinctive for their beliefs, or clothes, or diet, or language, or even their looks, the real problem – the common theme transcending times, places, and cultures – is their desperation. It may be a war back home, or a famine, or some form of social chaos, but the root cause is neither "their biology" nor "their culture." The problem is relational and geopolitical, and neither inherent in, nor possessed by, individual people or specific groups.

Consequently, racism is neither really biological nor cultural. It is neither a property of our genomes (in spite of naive scientists who imagine a naturalistic basis for "xenophobia"), nor the property of a group (in spite of the obvious ideologies of Nazis or Klansmen), but rather lies in the relations between human groups, whose compositions may be quite diverse. That is to say, it inheres in the historical, political, and economic relationship between Black and White, or English and Irish, or Australian and Aborigine, or Japanese and Korean, or Hutu and Tutsi. To talk about it as a "cultural" thing is misleading in that it reifies the phenomenon ("racism") that it seeks to analyze; the real sense in which racism is "cultural" is just the sad state of affairs in which there is no conceptual alternative to "natural."

The taxonomic fallacy has been the principal stumbling block to the successful widespread application of genetics for medicine. We think of race and disease within the constraints of contemporary bio-political ideas about health and the meaning of human differences. The eugenics movement, popular internationally in the first half of the twentieth century, brought sophisticated modern genetic science in to solve the social problems of the age, given some vulgar assumptions about the differential innate value of broad groups of people. In particular, eugenics rested on a nineteenth-century observation that poor people tend to out-breed rich people (Bashford and Levine, 2010).

We now know that reproductive rates are very sensitive to economic and other short-term local cultural variables. A hundred years ago, scientists were more struck by the implications of long-term differences in birth rates, assuming that the rapidly breeding poor were inferior – intellectually, constitutionally, morally, however you care to measure inferiority – and simple extrapolation predicted a future "swamped with incompetence."

In the 1920s, then, biomedical science was underpinned and unified by the idea that certain classes of people were less endowed genetically than others, and that a better class of citizen could be bred through the judicious regulation of marriage and reproduction. This, however, masked some intellectual diversity. In the UK, the movement was largely built on class prejudice, while in the US it was class- and race-based. Moreover, British eugenicists were primarily working on statistical models of the human gene pool, and were less interested in Mendelian units of heredity and their effects. In America, however, eugenics had a thoroughly Mendelian outlook, premised on the distribution of the imaginary gene for feeblemindedness (Kevles, 1985; Mazumdar, 1992).

A popular American genetics textbook of 1925 warned college students of "a great many people who are always on the border line of self-supporting existence and whose contribution to society is so small that the elimination of their stock would be beneficial" (Sinnott and Dunn, 1925). A German genetics textbook made similar points, but treated the Jews in greater depth (Baur et al., 1921). In both cases, obviously, local cultural values were being inscribed into the genetic science and read back out again. The medical metaphor was more explicit to the Germans, who abjured the term "eugenics" in favor of "race hygiene." The issue, though, was resonant across nations. What are we to do with large numbers of poor people? Can science help us?

The American writer Madison Grant obliged with *The Passing of the Great Race* (1916), which called for sterilization of the poor and restriction of immigration from southern and eastern Europe (code for Italians and Jews). While there were some private complaints about his racial radicalism, most of the American genetics community was content to serve under him in the American Eugenics Society. Madison Grant's book was reviewed favorably in *Science* (Woods, 1918) and engendered fan mail from both his friend (and fellow conservationist) Theodore Roosevelt and from the aspiring European politician (after the publication of the 1924 German translation) Adolf Hitler (Spiro, 2009).

By 1927, the US had an immigration restriction bill (which would prevent refugees from the Nazis from entering the country a few years later), and the Supreme Court had supported the right of states to sterilize the poor involuntarily (which would continue in some parts of the US into the 1970s). The sterilization laws had been drafted by a leading American eugenicist/ geneticist, Harry Laughlin. When the Nazis enacted their Nuremberg Laws in 1935, they honored the inspiration they had gotten from Laughlin by awarding him an honorary doctorate from Heidelberg University. (Even so, having the Nazis love you was sufficiently embarrassing that Laughlin was obliged to receive it at the German Embassy in New York.) When Nazi doctor Karl Brandt was tried at Nuremberg in 1948, he read excerpts from Madison Grant's book into the record, to show that he was only doing what the Americans had been advocating. He was hanged anyway. But he was right about the intellectual continuity between American genetics of the 1920s and German genetics of the 1930s (Kühl, 1994).

After World War II, the scientific study of human heredity had to be thoroughly reinvented, as we noted in Chapter 2. That reinvention partly involved writing the eugenics movement out of its history.

As a consequence, it is often difficult for modern geneticists to talk about the eugenics movement, which leaves four discursive strategies available. First, to ignore or marginalize it; after all, eugenics was wrong, and the history of science (as scientists like to relate it) is a timeline of right ideas. Second, to deny the involvement of the scientific community, and relegate the eugenics movement to cranks, charlatans, and amateurs, like Madison Grant. Except that, even though Grant himself was not a credentialed scientist, he certainly saw eye-to-eye with the leading American scientists, who praised his book and worked alongside and under him at the American Eugenics Society. Third, to deny any relationship between the past and present; after all, that was then and this is now. And we certainly wouldn't want to learn anything from the bad geneticists of the past, would we? And fourth, why are you bringing this up anyway; are you anti-science? (This is particularly resonant in the context of creationism, given that the first three presidents of the British Eugenics Society were, respectively and possibly embarrassingly, Darwin's cousin, Darwin's son, and the leading evolutionary geneticist in England.)

Failing to engage substantively with the eugenics movement, however, indeed has had a subsequent impact upon the human genetics community. Even while reframing the ambitions and methods of human genetics, there often remains a genetic desideratum – partly humanitarian, partly utopian, partly totalitarian – to cure illness and improve the world. But there are two problems here. First, illness is not quite so easy to define genetically. Given that Tay–Sachs is and feeble-mindedness isn't, what about slowness of foot? That is being marketed as a genetic test in the burgeoning direct-to-consumer arena. Or schizophrenia or alcoholism or homosexuality or lack of faith in God – all of which have been presumptively identified in the genome, by geneticists? And second, once you have identified a genetic illness, what is to be done about it? Sterilization? Abortion? Non-existent gene therapy? Stigmatization?

That last one – stigmatization – was indeed one of the major consequences of the American sickle-cell screening program in the 1970s. Targeted at the African-American population, which is disproportionately affected by the genetic disease, the screening program had humanitarian ideals quite different from human realities. The test could not distinguish between (asymptomatic) carriers of sickle-cell anemia and actual victims, who presumably already knew that they had a serious health problem. If one of those asymptomatic carriers has a child with another asymptomatic carrier (there is about a one in thirteen chance of that in the African-American community for the sickle-cell carrier), and there is a one in four chance that the child will have sickle-cell anemia, then what is to be done? Abort? Sterilize? Counsel them not to breed? The Nobel Laureate chemist Linus Pauling was infamously clear in 1968: "There should be tattooed on the forehead of every young person, a symbol showing possession of the sickle cell gene [so as to prevent] two young people carrying the same seriously defective gene in single dose from falling in love with one another" (see Duster, 1990).

The screening program was not particularly successful, which is understandable, given what the scientists said they wanted to do to the people they were looking for. Moreover, the sickle-cell screening program was proceeding at just the time that the "Tuskegee experiment" was being exposed – a 40-year project that ran from 1932 to 1972, spanning the Nazis and the development of penicillin, in which poor black men in Alabama with syphilis were studied, but not treated. And further, geneticists were still calling the sickle-cell program "eugenic," which now meant something along the lines of: "We want to do something positive for the gene pool of the black community, which doesn't involve killing or sterilizing anybody like we used to advocate, just wantonly spreading some shame and guilt and at worst some public humiliation" (see Wailoo and Pemberton, 2006; Washington, 2006; Comfort, 2012).

In fact, all groups of people have their own genetic idiosyncrasies, as a result of their unique histories, but they do not map on to race. For example, northern

Europeans are at greater risk from cystic fibrosis than southern Europeans, and sickle-cell anemia is associated with Old World populations at risk from malaria, which includes a broader region than just tropical Africa, and places Saudis and Indians at genetic risk as well. Ashkenazi Jews and French Canadians are at high risk from Tay–Sachs disease, South African Boers from variegated porphyria, and Pennsylvania Amish from Ellis-van Creveld Syndrome – yet none of these maps onto modern ideas of race; they are simply groups of people with common identities and histories. Indeed to racialize these genetic data would simply be to confuse them terribly.

Although primarily a burden on the African American community, sickle-cell anemia is a fairly minor health issue, given that health issues with more physiologically complex etiologies affect blacks and whites in America disproportionately – for example, the probability of having low-birthweight babies (in black women) and hypertension (in black men). Overall, there is a four-year difference in average life expectancy between blacks and whites. This difference, like that between people living in the north and south of England, or Mississippi and Vermont in the US, is universally understood to be the result of social and economic inequalities.

All groups of people have their particular health issues, sometimes a consequence of their history, but more often a consequence of where they live, what they do, and what they experience, on the average. The demonstration in 1775 that British chimney sweeps were particularly prone to scrotal cancer provides an origin myth for social epidemiology, which began to flourish in the mid-nineteenth century, identifying health risks in (often poor, urban) local communities. Today, the health hazards of living near a toxic waste dump, or having a job that requires repetitive motions, are universally acknowledged. In the modern age, carefully controlled studies have shown that complex racial health problems like elevated risks of low-birthweight babies (David and Collins, 1997) and hypertension (Kaufman and Hall, 2003) are best understood as a consequence of growing up black in America, or "embodiment" (Wade, 2004; Krieger, 2005). Focusing on the genome makes it possible to ignore the social conditions that cause most of the health disparities.

Another way of ignoring the social conditions that cause health disparities is to dismiss the etiology altogether, and simply treat the symptom pharmaceutically. This involves the creation of racial "niche markets" for new drugs. If the groups are already presumed to differ naturalistically, then it becomes that much easier to imagine a drug that could be specific to one. (What we actually know about human variation strongly indicates that pharmaceutical interventions should be targeted to individual genotypes, for which racial groups are very imperfect proxies and would directly result in a very large number of mis-prescribed medicines.) The vanguard was a heart medicine called BiDil, which was approved by the US Food and Drug Administration in 2005 specifically for African American patients, on the basis of no valid epidemiological data that it worked better or differently in African Americans than in anyone else. It did extend the private patent protection for the drug, but eventually drove the company to financial disaster, because they grossly overpriced it. BiDil, you see, was never a public health measure, but a profitmaking venture. It did nothing to ameliorate the very real health differences between blacks and whites in America, which are almost entirely attributable to social and economic causes, but did crassly exploit those differences in order to profiteer from the people who actually needed the medical intervention (Kahn, 2012; Pollock, 2012).

The theme that unifies these stories – from the eugenic science of the 1920s to the commodified genomic science of today – is the mistaken belief that human races are naturalistic categories equivalent to units that are familiar zoologically. And that is precisely what human groups are not. Indeed, just compared to our closest relatives, there are no two living human groups that stand in the same relationship to one another as the way in which *Pan troglodytes verus* and *Pan troglodytes schweinfurthii* stand to one another. Human groups are bounded culturally and symbolically; they are units of identity and narratives of kinship. The taxonomic fallacy of race is to imagine that these units, which seem to be like biological taxa, are more like Felidae or Aves or *Brachyteles hypoxanthus* than they are like the dollar or the Arsenal Football Club or atheism. Those are all real, but not in a biological, genetically testable sense. One could, of course, study the gene pool of atheists, a sports team, or dollar users, but why bother? Those data would have a naturalistic meaning that is subtle at best. Human groups are not composed in ways that are readily accessible to biological or genetic analysis, because their boundaries are not founded in biology or genetics. That's why we "need" things like endogamy rules and caste systems and miscegenation laws – to reinforce the cultural divisions that are represented at best subtly in the gene pool.

In June 2015, three stories circulated simultaneously across American news spaces, chat groups, and social media sites. In the first, a local political activist in

Spokane, Washington, was discovered to be misrepresenting herself as black, although she was born white and had white biological parents. Black was an identity that she adopted as an adult – and would have continued with, had her own parents not "outed" her. In the second, a 9,500-year-old skeleton, discovered twenty years earlier, was found to be genetically more closely allied to modern Native Americans than to Europeans, despite the protestations of scientists who had maintained that it was European-looking, and thus not a sacred ancestor of Native Americans. In the third, a 21-year-old white supremacist named Dylann Roof murdered nine black people in a church in Charleston, South Carolina – leading to a nationwide referendum on the Confederate flag and to a wave of arson against African American churches. And shortly thereafter, videos of American policemen physically abusing or killing black citizens who appeared vaguely threatening inspired the slogan and hashtag "#BlackLivesMatter." These facts are difficult to reconcile with the claim that modern society is "post-racial." But they certainly show that racial issues are social and political, not biological.

FIVE

What we know, and why it matters

The question posed in the title of this book has a deceptively simple answer. Science is racist to the extent that its practitioners may be narrowly trained and particularly shielded from the knowledge about race that differs from their folk knowledge or common sense. But much of the advancement of science emerges from demonstrating how common sense is wrong: the sun doesn't go around the earth, even though it appears to; water isn't elemental and indivisible, it is composed of colorless and odorless gases; and human groups are not fundamental biological divisions of the species, they are clusters of people linked together in arbitrary cultural ways.

Not being a formal scientific concept, a human race is largely not accessible to the scientist. It can only be grasped through the humanities: historically, experientially, politically. The crucial advance comes with the recognition after World War II that human variation is amenable to scientific analysis, and does not yield results that map onto race. Are Africans different biologically from Europeans? Of course, but East Africans are different from West Africans, and Nigerian Ibos are different from Nigerian Yorubas. Race is not difference – because all human groups differ from each other, as do all human beings. Race involves imposing some cultural patterns upon human differences.

Having thus differentiated human variation from race, let us summarize the positive knowledge we have about them and their relationship to one another.

1 Human groups distinguish themselves principally culturally

Telling one group from another is boundary work, and the boundaries of human groups are rarely, if ever, naturalistic (Peregrine et al., 2003). Blacks "passing" for white have been well known (and feared) for centuries, and recent cases of whites "passing" for black or Native American have become familiar. How were they able to get away with it? By "talking the talk" and "walking the walk" – that is to say, by assimilating the behavior, speech, interests, and identities of non-whites – in defiance of their physical appearance or DNA. They got away with it because we know, certainly in boundary cases – that looks can be deceiving. Human identities are sometimes based on biology – consider the bonds established by people who share a genetic disease (Rapp et al., 2001).

By focusing on patterns of cultural diversity, however, we replicate the biology–culture dichotomy that we would like to transcend, but the message is crucial. Humans distinguish themselves from others whom they perceive as unlike them predominantly by symbolic markers like speech, dress, grooming, beliefs, and taboos, and not by properties of the genotype or phenotype. To the extent that there are biological distinctions, these are sufficiently subtle that they require cultural augmentation or elaboration to be effective.

2 There is much more variation within groups (polymorphism) than between groups (polytypy)

One of the logical consequences of acknowledging that human races are established and bounded primarily culturally is that their apparent and commonsensical patterns ought to be quite different from their detectable biological patterns. The biological reality of race could be supported by the discovery that presumptive races were generally homogeneous, and qualitatively different from their neighbors. But we find the opposite: presumptive races are very heterogeneous genetically, and can't be easily distinguished from their neighbors genetically. There are, of course, biological differences among groups of people. We call that pattern of difference – the differences between groups – polytypy. But the amount of heterogeneity within any group, or polymorphism, considerably dwarfs the amount of detectable polytypy.

That fact was known crudely even before World War II, but in the 1970s geneticists were able to quantify it, and to show that, at most, only about 15 percent of the detectable genetic variation was polytypic. Consider, for example, the ABO blood group, where nearly all human populations have all three major alleles, and O is always the most common one, but its frequency ranges from about 50 percent to over 95 percent, depending upon what people you are studying. A Native American is more likely to have type O blood than a native Australian, but someone with type O blood could be from either group – because the relevant genetic variation is ubiquitous. Most genetic variation in our species turns out to be patterned that way. Whatever genetic markers you look at, 85–95 percent of the variation that geneticists can find is polymorphic. That is to say, the variants are cosmopolitan, they are found nearly everywhere, and differ only in their proportions across human populations.

This is a different pattern than racial theory would predict, in which the fundamental divisions of our species ought to be relatively few and relatively discrete (Graves, 2004; Tattersall and DeSalle, 2011). That is similar to what we see in chimpanzees, but not in humans.

3 Human biological variation is continuous, not discrete

Human populations intergrade with one another (Handley et al., 2007). The continuous pattern of human variation (in contrast to the general discontinuity in patterns of race and culture) was recognized by scholars in the eighteenth century. The allure of the new-fangled biological taxonomy as applied to human beings was so strong that the anatomist Johann Friedrich Blumenbach could write that human populations intergrade so insensibly with one another than it is impossible to mark out the boundaries between them – before proceeding to do just that. (Blumenbach's contribution to Western civilization was his aesthetic judgment that the most beautiful skulls in Europe came from the inhabitants of the Caucasus mountains, as a result of which he called the European peoples "Caucasians.")

While human cultural variation is largely boundary work, human biological variation is patterned quite differently, whether examined in the body or the DNA. The discreteness that so often identifies a person as a member of a tribe, clan, nation, cult, or race is no longer detectable in the data of biology.

The reason is that human populations are in genetic contact with one another, as a result of social, economic, military, or other kinds of cultural relations between them. The "isolated" population is a classic colonial myth, for isolation is a relative term, and an absolutely isolated human population would perforce rapidly become an extinct human population (Wolf, 1982). Unfortunately, although geneticists have been quick to acknowledge the genetic contact of populations, it is easier to model population histories by denying that contact. So when population geneticists appealed to the public in the 1990s for a Big Science program to study human population histories genetically – in a Human Genome Diversity Project – they incorporated an imaginative background of isolation for those populations. That is one of the reasons the project did not receive the major funding it sought (Reardon, 2004).

4 Populations are biologically real, not races

The development of population genetics in the 1930s introduced a new degree of mathematical rigor to ecological and evolutionary studies. By the 1950s the study of real groups of human beings (i.e., populations) had supplanted the study of idealized human subspecies, each with their own distinct properties (Yudell, 2014).

Racial theorists transiently navigated the shift from imaginary racial essences to real human populations by simply calling their races "populations." Really, really big populations. But the reality of a human population is grounded in its local, rather than its global or para-continental distribution (Thieme, 1952; Johnston, 1966). The units of human adaptation are narrow; there is no "climate of Africa" to adapt to. Environments are neighborhoods. Even with broad stressors, most notably malaria, what is relevant is the distribution of the disease, which is neither exclusive to Africa, nor pan-African. Racializing the genetic responses to it neither illuminates, nor is illuminated by, the actual epidemiology.

This is not to say that the concept of "human population" is easy to operationalize. In humans, again, it may represent an identity based on beliefs that may or may not coincide well with a geographical community (Hauskeller et al., 2013). The human condition is thus unlike the condition of pocket gophers or lemurs, where one is really dealing with a geographically bounded community of mates and competitors for mates, not a group of geographically dispersed yet like-minded pocket gophers or lemurs.

As noted in the last chapter, although human races lack biological coherence or reality, the consequences of racism have very real effects upon human groups.

5 Populations also have a constructed component

The primary patterns of human diversity are cultural, polymorphic, clinal, and local. To study human diversity is to study aspects of these patterns; to study race is to study something else, namely the imposition of meaningful categorical difference upon this variation, and its consequent impact upon people's lives. And unlike populations of fruit flies, populations of human beings inherit and adopt roles and identities that guide them in associating with other conspecifics. But they also find ways of subverting those identities and adopting new ones, for many reasons: economic, geographical, emotional. People intermarry with their neighbors, whom they are supposed to hate, or move to a new place and become absorbed into the group and gene pool (Cabana and Clark, 2011).

Moreover, identities themselves evolve, passing into and out of existence (McAnany and Yoffee, 2009). Hittites comprised an important identity in the Near East three thousand years ago, but no longer, although they certainly have descendants alive today. Their descendants simply have other identities. These identities are thus partly naturalistic (for being geographically localized) and partly symbolic (for being units of political salience). From a strictly genetical viewpoint, human populations are very porous.

This also means that no human population is genetically pure. Purity, after all, implies extreme inbreeding, which is generally enfeebling for a population.

6 Clustering populations is arbitrary

The units of the human gene pool are local, but races are presumably para-continental. Could we bridge this conceptual gap by imagining that a para-continental race is just a large assemblage of local populations?

We might, if we had some objective way of knowing which populations to assemble, and where to stop and to start a different assemblage. The short cut of taking, say, the peoples of sub-Saharan Africa and assembling them as an African "race" simply imposes the common-sensical or folk category upon the data. It assumes race rather than discovers race.

Indeed, one of the earliest conceptual problems faced by racial theorists in the early twentieth century was the subdivision of the "major" races into "minor" races. After all, a tall, blond Scandinavian can be distinguished from a short, swarthy Sicilian nearly as efficiently as the Scandinavian can be distinguished from a Ugandan. Thus, trying to grapple with clinal human variation simply among Europeans, but limited conceptually to a Linnaean taxonomic framework, William Z. Ripley in 1899 formalized the existence of three races within the European race: Teutonic (Nordic), Alpine, and Mediterranean. As noted in Chapter 2, a revision of Ripley's work in 1939 saw many more than three races of Europeans. If you have no guidelines for doing so, you can divide the human species up infinitesimally, which was quickly recognized to beggar the credulity of having these divisions represent "natural" clusters of Europeans. In parallel, fieldworkers in Africa began to speak of the "races of Africa," again substituting an

odd-sounding plural for the more familiar and commonsensical singular.

The geneticist or biologist can study similarity and
difference between, say, the Irish and the Spanish, but
cannot say whether those differences represent two variations on a common theme, so to speak, or two separate
themes. And once we appreciate that the human species
can be endlessly subdivided, because the acts of dividing
and summing people are ultimately arbitrary, we can
see why attempts to tally up the human races scientifically have ranged from two (straight- and curly-haired)
to the dozens. There is in fact no correct number of
naturalistic groupings of human beings (Keevak, 2011).

7 People are similar to those nearby and different from those far away

Given the clinal nature of human biological variation,
it should not be surprising that the best predictor of
how similar two populations are would be their geographical proximity to one another. This is a simple
consequence of the fact that people are more likely to
intermarry with people nearby than with people far
away. Consequently, perceptions of race – experienced
as discontinuity, or discrete differences – are generally

linked to historical patterns of immigration from distant places.

Although the generalization that geography is the best predictor of genetic similarity holds, this generalization entails an odd assumption. As well-attested and obvious a fact as this may be, it may not actually apply to you. It certainly does not apply to me. I write these words in Charlotte, North Carolina, and there is absolutely no relationship between the relatedness and proximity of my neighbors to me. After all, I moved to Charlotte barely sixteen years ago and have only one blood relative here.

And without getting into wherever the heck my ancestors were living 150 years ago, it certainly wasn't in North Carolina. And my ancestors 500 years ago were nowhere even near North America. The generalization about ancestry and geography only pertains to indigenous peoples, not to the people of the world who have participated in the demographic movements brought on by the forces of colonialism and industrialism. This is a solid, but romanticized, generalization about a pre-Columbian world, where Australia is populated solely by Aborigines, America by Native Americans, and there were no Asians in California or Africans in the Caribbean. This is a vision of the world arbitrarily historical and considerably disconnected from the realities of the urban and genetic modern world (Cartmill, 1998).

When recreational genomic ancestry tests tell you information about your geographical ancestry, what they are actually summarizing is your genetic similarity to the DNA they have collected from discrete and distant indigenous populations. Customers seem to regard this as "science lite," accepting conclusions they like and dismissing or ignoring conclusions that they don't like. That seems reasonable.

8 Racial classification is historical and political, and does not reflect natural biological patterns

Here we turn to history and ethnography to see the ways in which races have been encoded differently and how inherently unstable this classification is. In merely comparing the US and UK census forms, we can observe that the first category is the same for both: "White." But the US form leaves it simple and undifferenti-ated, calling it a race, while the UK (tabulating "ethnic groups") distinguishes "English/Welsh/Northern Irish/ British" from "Irish." The UK subcategory "Gypsy or Irish Traveller" makes as little sense to an American ear as "Neptunian" might. Where the American form leaves "Black, African Am., or Negro" undifferentiated, the UK form separates Caribbean from African. Most significant is the treatment of Asians, for whom the US form differentiates among the nations of east Asia, but not south Asia; and the UK form does the opposite, differentiating Indians, Pakistanis, and Bangladeshis, but naming Chinese as the only category of east Asians. And the catchall US category "Some other race – Print race" becomes "Other ethnic group" in the UK, and helpfully specifies "Arab" as a possible answer.

On both sides of the Atlantic, no matter what you call them, these are units of political salience, not of nature – and their connection is to folk ideas about genetic similarity, rather than to empirical genetic patterns (Tutton et al., 2010). The UK form acknowledges as much, since, even though it is requesting the same information, it specifies "ethnic group," whereas the US form attempts to maintain the fiction that its categories are drawn from nature as "race." Especially confusing is that the US census form separates the "Hispanic, Latino, or Spanish origin" question from the race question, on the reasonable grounds that "Hispanic" is asking what language your ancestors spoke, not necessarily what they looked like. It unites people of distinct heritages: "Hispanic" in California usually connotes recent Mexican ancestry; while in Florida it usually connotes recent Cuban ancestry. Yet many of the people who answer that they are Hispanic then proceed to skip the "Race" question, figuring that it is redundant. Moreover, the US form is notably unhelpful to Brazilian immigrants, who may be considered "Latino" without being "Hispanic."

Over the course of the twentieth century, European groups who had been traditionally racialized – namely the Irish and the Jews – became absorbed into the American category "White." White, after all, is a metaphor for skin color, essentially mapping onto "European" geographically and "Caucasian" cranio-facially. The expansion of "White" to include Jews and Irish in America is currently being mirrored in a reciprocal shrinkage, so as to exclude Hispanics and Middle Eastern Muslims. This again helps to show how racism is prior to race. The political act does not depend upon the natural divisions of the human species, but, rather, constructs, bounds, and reifies those divisions (Wade, 2002).

9 Humans have little genetic variation

Although the human and chimpanzee lineages are each about six million years old, the chimpanzee gene pool harbors considerably more genetic variation than the human gene pool does. This is a counterintuitive discovery, given that chimpanzees are all found in a localized part of Africa and all seem pretty similar, and humans are all over the world and seem so different.

And yet, compare two chimpanzees and two humans from anywhere, and the chimps will be much more different from one another. The same holds for gorillas, which suggests that something noteworthy has happened to the human gene pool, namely a considerable contraction. There are two causes for this loss of genetic diversity. The first is the long-term action of natural selection, elevating the frequency of one gene variant over others, and losing the others in the process. Over generations, the favored gene sequence, and the DNA surrounding it, sweep away the alternative genetic variants in the gene pool. And although we can't identify the genetic regions involved, there has certainly been a lot of selection involved in our separation from the apes: our mode of sound production, our cognitive symbolic thought processes, prosociality, bipedality, heat dissipation, and dexterity, to label just a few.

The other mechanism by which species can lose their genetic diversity is through the random effects of genetic drift, caused by population bottlenecks, or just the long-term effects of having small populations. And that is precisely the demographic situation that we believe to have predominated among our ancestors: living in small, mobile bands of hunter-gatherers.

Whatever the cause, then, a division into biologically or genetically well-differentiated groups seems to be a feature of the chimpanzee gene pool, but not of the human. Not only does our species not have much between-group genetic variation, but we have little genetic variation at all (Enard and Pääbo, 2004).

10 Racial issues are social-political-economic, not biological

Racial issues only exist because of the unequal social privileges that accrue by virtue of having been classified. In a post-Enlightenment democratic republic of the modern age, we recognize that social equality is desirable, and that, in the ways that sexism parallels racism, so men, women, blacks, and whites should all be social equals. But men tend to enjoy more social privileges than women, and people of European ancestry enjoy more privileges than people of African ancestry. We see this as a historical legacy of the politics of patriarchy and colonialism, in which case, as noted in Chapter 1, the solution is to work for social justice. Science ought to be more or less irrelevant.

But, as we also noted, there is a counter-argument, which holds that the inequality is not unjust, for the social inequality is rooted in an underlying inequality of nature, that simply remains to be discovered. The recruitment of science for this end is what we mean by the term "scientific racism" and it is fueled by the spread of ignorance about human biology. Historians who study the deliberate perpetuation of ignorance call their field "agnotology" (Proctor and Schiebinger, 2008). It applies very aptly to the dissimulation that imaginary natural differences in ability are at the root of social inequalities. Moreover, difference is a quantitative genetic state, and we are all different, while equality is a political state, and we are all equal; the two states are disconnected from one another. People should be accorded equal rights regardless of their genotype.

The irrelevant scientific element that is most politically seductive is hereditarianism, or the idea that innate, inherited qualities determine crucial aspects of one's life course. After all, as we noted in Chapter 2, identical twins reared apart have the most extraordinary similarities – marrying women with the same name, giving their dogs the same name, twitching nervously the same way – which surely proves the dominance of the genes. (At least to the very credulous.) The (pseudo-)knowledge that there is a mostly genetic basis for differences in intelligence and personality implies that social inequality, which is mostly the result of intellectual and personality traits, is mostly genetic. And thus, social equality can never be achieved, for it is limited by the invisible barriers to intellectual improvement – so it is not worth working toward, and governments ought to direct their priorities elsewhere. This is an odious updated version of social Darwinism, familiar to critical readers of *The Bell Curve* (1994), and requiring the active participation of scientists – in this case psychologists – to confuse folk ideologies with scientific knowledge.

And there are, in fact, political philanthropies whose goal is to legitimize and promote the idea that different peoples have different natures. In Chapter 1, for example, we noted the work of psychologist J. Philippe Rushton, whose ideas about human biology, evolution, and intelligence were not simply racist, but idiotically so – that Asians evolved biologically to be law-abiding, highly intellectualized, and poorly sexualized, manifested physically in large brains and small penises as the naturalistic opposites of Africans – and yet there are still psychologists who casually cite his work as if that were not a problem. Scientific racism is intellectually corrupting.

In his bestseller, *Germs, Guns, and Steel* (1997), the renowned biologist Jared Diamond attempted to turn the tables on his imagined racist interlocutors by suggesting that New Guinea tribesman may actually be innately intellectually superior to Europeans, by virtue of the effects of natural selection for mental abilities. Diamond was making an argument drawn from political correctness, that "the usual racist assumption has to be turned on its head." However, the solution is not to replace it with an *unusual* racist assumption, but to replace it with no racist solution at all. The argument that different groups of people have different innate intellectual powers, such that a randomly drawn person from one population is likely to be inherently more strongly endowed mentally than a random person from another population, is a racist argument – regardless of which population is placed on the top of the ladder.

Human evolution is now understood as having produced a brain of considerable plasticity and adaptability, allowing its bearers to communicate, socialize, and thrive effectively in diverse fashions and places. Intelligence is a nebulous concept at best, and whatever genetic variation that underpins it cannot be delimited in a sufficiently precise way as to produce meaningful comparisons across populations. This is, of course, not to say that all people are the same, nor that all populations are the same – merely that whatever genetic variation might exist in the normal range of the human species (excluding savants and the brain-damaged) is quite simply overwhelmed by the diverse conditions of life. Those differences in social and historical facts of life in the modern world are what need to be equilibrated. Any talk of imaginary alleles or imaginary regimes of selection for intellectual powers is a dissimulation, and distracts us from solving the very real problems of social inequality in our time.

Certainly, the most frustrating suggestion within the scientific community is the condescending acknowledgment of a fear that somehow the racial knowledge they expect to uncover might be somehow dangerous and potentially subject to abuse. But this assumes that scientific knowledge about the human condition exists abstractly and value-neutrally, either for beneficial application or for abuse (presumably meaning an application you retrospectively don't like). The basic reason that separation is illusory is that racist assumptions infuse the production of knowledge of human variation. The history of science shows this clearly: the eugenics movement in the 1920s and 1930s was not a corruption of scientific ideas, it was an implementation of those ideas, in precisely the way that the scientists themselves had been consistently calling for in scholarly forums – for example, the *Journal of Heredity*. The fact that the scientists later changed their minds does not alter the quality of the earlier science.

Likewise, the *American Journal of Physical Anthropology* was founded in 1918 and remains a leading scientific journal on the subject of human diversity. But in its early decades, it published many papers that documented ways in which the heads of non-Europeans were inferior to those of Europeans. The field evolved; we now regard that early work as racist shit. Researchers framed their projects, collected data, and interpreted the results with the background knowledge of white supremacy; and in science, it is a truism that it is always easy to see what you are expecting to find.

So there is no fear of potential abuse of knowledge. There is simply the collection and dissemination of intellectually corrupted information. That is the legacy of scientific racism.

The making of racial knowledge, says a powerful analogy, is like the making of witchcraft (Fields and Fields, 2012). They are both real and obvious and logical and constantly being made; and yet not facts of nature at all, but agreed-upon facts of a particular age and place, whose activity and responses to their activity are real enough to maintain livelihoods, and to ruin or end lives, yet not quite so real as to sustain the rational scrutiny of the modern age.

Most importantly, the causes of social inequality are to be found in human economic practices, not in race; and so are the remedies. Indeed, when a prominent science journalist made that familiar hereditarian proposal in a recent bestseller – that Jews had genes disposing them to capitalism and the like – nearly 150 population geneticists signed a letter to the *New York Times* repudiating his presentation of human genetics (Coop et al., 2014). There's progress.

In sum, then, human groups differ from one another, but not in ways that the theory of race would predict. Science is racist when it embraces folk knowledge of human diversity and uses it as a substitute for scholarly expertise. To study human variation is to study the natural patterns by which people differ from one another. To study race, on the other hand, is to study the causes, methods, and consequences of classifying and stratifying human groups. Race is not the discovery of difference; it is the imposition of difference. Race is powerful and real, yet nevertheless an empirical biological falsehood. This is not to disparage the scientific study of human variation, which is valuable, but to shield it from racism; much as one would wish to shield the scientific study of human origins from creationism.

Chapter 1 Introduction

1 A discussion of science is going to be put off until Chapter 3. For present purposes, I will simply be using the word "science" to refer to the production of authoritative knowledge in the modern world.

2 http://www.nytimes.com/2014/04/12/opinion/sunday/raising-a-moral-child.html.

3 http://www.sfgate.com/science/article/Nobel-Winner-s-Theories-Raise-Uproar-in-Berkeley-3236584.php.

4 Vulcan is the "Star Trek" planet, notable for the overbearing logical thought of its inhabitants.

5 The journal *Human Biology* devoted much of its issue of Summer 2014 to critical reviews of the book.

6 Matthew 24:5.

Chapter 3 Science, race, and genomics

1 The call to remove the experimenter from the analysis is so powerful that young scientists are often instructed to write in the passive voice – "the temperature was raised," rather than "I raised the temperature" – to make it seem rhetorically as if the experimenter's presence is so irrelevant that it can safely be ignored.

2 Each one of the septillion ancestors recurs many times in the actual pedigree, reflecting how inbred we all are.

3 This is about the human population in the Neolithic, which was not large by modern standards, but was certainly considerably larger than two, despite the coincidence of the age calculated for the common ancestry of living people with the age of the cosmos assumed by "young-earth creationists."

4 All quotations are taken from the oxfordancestors.com website.

5 The cultural anthropologist Paul Rabinow has called the construction of fictive kin relations on the basis of ostensibly natural data "bio-sociality."

Chapter 4 Racism and biomedical science

1 This is distinct from the general practices of taxonomic "lumping" (into few species) and "splitting" (into many species). Nor is it to say that zoological species are unproblematic and objective units of nature; in fact, they are often subject to political and economic inputs of various kinds (Kirksey, 2015). My point is simply that those "species" are not units of our ancestry narrative, and are different from, and not comparable to, the "species" that do compose our origin story.

2 Claude Lévi-Strauss (1962) used the term "bricolage" to refer to the available elements a mythmaker draws on, while tinkering to construct a resonant story. It was borrowed by molecular biologist François Jacob (1977) to argue that evolution is more like a tinkerer than like an engineer.

Abu El-Haj, N. (2012) *The Genealogical Science: The Search for Jewish Origins and the Politics of Epistemology.* Chicago: University of Chicago Press.

Ackermann, R. R., Mackay, A., and Arnold, M. L. (2016) The hybrid origin of "modern" humans. *Evolutionary Biology*, 43: 1–11.

Anonymous [Chambers, R.] (1844) *Vestiges of the Natural History of Creation.* London: John Churchill.

Barash, D. P. (1995) Book review: Race, Evolution, and Behavior. *Animal Behaviour*, 49: 1131–1133.

Bashford, A. and Levine, P., eds. (2010) *The Oxford Handbook of the History of Eugenics.* New York: Oxford University Press.

Baur, E., Fischer, E., and Lenz, F. (1921) *Grundriss der menschlichen Erblichkeitslehre und Rassenhygiene.* Munich: J. F. Lehmanns.

Boyd, W. C. (1963) Genetics and the human race. *Science*, 140: 1057–1065.

Cabana, G. S. and Clark, J. J., eds. (2011) *Rethinking Anthropological Perspectives on Migration.* Gainesville: University of Florida Press.

Cartmill, M. (1998) The status of the race concept in physical anthropology. *American Anthropologist*, 100: 651–660.

Chase, A. (1977) *The Legacy of Malthus: The Social Costs of the New Scientific Racism.* Urbana: University of Illinois Press.

Comfort, N. (2012) *The Science of Human Perfection: How Genes Became the Heart of American Medicine.* New Haven: Yale University Press.

References

Coon, C. S. (1939) *The Races of Europe*. New York: Macmillan.

Coop, G. et al. (2014) Letters: "A Troublesome Inheritance." *New York Times Sunday Book Review*, August 8.

David, R. J. and Collins, J. W., Jr. (1997) Differing birth weights among infants of US-born blacks, African-born blacks, and US-born whites. *New England Journal of Medicine*, 337: 1209–1214.

Diamond, J. M. (1997) *Guns, Germs, and Steel: The Fates of Human Societies*. New York: W. W. Norton.

Dobzhansky, T. (1962) Genetics and equality. *Science*, 137: 112–115.

Duster, T. (1990) *Backdoor to Eugenics*. New York: Routledge.

Enard, W. and Pääbo, S. (2004) Comparative primate genomics. *Annual Review of Genomics and Human Genetics*, 5: 351–378.

Evans, P., Gilbert, S., Mekel-Bobrov, N., Vallender, E., Anderson, J., Vaez-Azizi, L., Tishkoff, S., Hudson, R., and Lahn, B. (2005) Microcephalin, a gene regulating brain size, continues to evolve adaptively in humans. *Science*, 309: 1717–1720.

Fabian, A. (2010) *The Skull Collectors: Race, Science, and America's Unburied Dead*. Chicago: University of Chicago Press.

Fields, B. and Fields, K. (2012) *Racecraft: The Soul of Inequality in American Life*. New York: Verso.

Fish, J., ed. (2001) *Race and Intelligence: Separating Science from Myth*. Mahwah: Lawrence Erlbaum.

Graeber, D. (2011) *Debt: The First 5,000 Years*. New York: Melville House.

Grant, M. (1916) *The Passing of the Great Race*. New York: Scribner's.

Graves, J. (2004) *The Race Myth: Why We Pretend Race Exists in America*. New York: Dutton.

Haeckel, E. (1868/1892) *The History of Creation*, trans. R. Lankester, 4th edn. London: Kegan Paul, Trench, Trübner and Co.

References

Handley, L. J. L., Manica, A., Goudet, J., and Balloux, F. (2007) Going the distance: human population genetics in a clinal world. *Trends in Genetics*, 23: 432–439.

Hauskeller, C., Sturdy, S., and Tutton, R. (2013) Genetics and the sociology of identity. *Sociology*, 47: 875–886.

Herrnstein, R. and Murray, C. (1994) *The Bell Curve*. New York: Free Press.

Holden, C. (1980) Identical twins reared apart. *Science*, 207: 1323–1328.

Holden, C. (1987) The genetics of personality. *Science*, 237: 598–601.

Holden, C. (2009) Behavioral geneticist celebrates twins, scorns PC science. *Science*, 325: 27.

Hooton, E. A. (1946) *Up from the Ape*, 2nd ed. New York: Macmillan.

Hrdlička, A. (1908) Physical anthropology and its aims. *Science*, 28: 41–42.

Hrdlička, A. (1930) Human races. In *Human Biology and Racial Welfare*, ed. E. W. Cowdry. New York: Paul B. Hoeber.

Hunt-Grubbe, C. (2007) The elementary DNA of Dr. Watson. *The Sunday Times (London)*, October 14.

Huxley, T. H. (1865 [1901]) Emancipation – black and white. In *Man's Place in Nature, and Other Anthropological Essays*. New York: Macmillan.

Jacob, F. (1977) Evolution and tinkering. *Science*, 196: 1161–1166.

Jaroff, L. (1989) The gene hunt. *Time Magazine*, March 20.

Jobling, M. A. (2012) The impact of recent events on human genetic diversity. *Philosophical Transactions of the Royal Society*, Series B 367: 793–799.

Johnston, F. E. (1966) The population approach to human variation. *Annals of the New York Academy of Sciences*, 134: 507–515.

Kahn, J. (2012) *Race in a Bottle: The Story of BiDil and Racialized Medicine in a Post-Genomic Age*. New York: Columbia University Press.

Kaufman, J. and Hall, S. (2003) The slavery hypertension hypothesis: dissemination and appeal of a modern race theory. *Epidemiology and Society*, 14: 111–126.

Keevak, M. (2011) *Becoming Yellow: A Short History of Racial Thinking*. Princeton: Princeton University Press.

Kevles, D. J. (1985) *In the Name of Eugenics*. Berkeley: University of California Press.

Kirksey, E. (2015) Species: A praxigraphic study. *Journal of the Royal Anthropological Institute*, 21: 758–780.

Krieger, N. (2005) Embodiment: a conceptual glossary for epidemiology. *Journal of Epidemiology and Community Health*, 59: 350–355.

Lahn, B. T. and Ebenstein, L. (2009) Let's celebrate human genetic diversity. *Nature*, 461: 726–728.

Lancaster, R. N. (2003) *The Trouble with Nature: Sex in Science and Popular Culture*. Berkeley: University of California Press.

Kühl, S. (1994) *The Nazi Connection*. New York: Oxford University Press.

Landau, M. (1991) *Narratives of Human Evolution*. New Haven: Yale University Press.

Lee, S., Bolnick, D., Duster, T., Ossorio, P., and TallBear, K. (2009) The illusive gold standard in genetic ancestry testing. *Science*, 325: 38.

Lévi-Strauss, C. (1962) *The Savage Mind*. Chicago: University of Chicago Press.

Lewontin, R. C. (1972) The apportionment of human diversity. *Evolutionary Biology*, 6: 381–398.

Livingstone, D. (2008) *Adam's Ancestors: Race, Religion, and the Politics of Human Origins*. Baltimore: Johns Hopkins University Press.

References

Manias, C. (2009) The race prussienne controversy: scientific internationalism and the nation. *Isis*, 100: 733–757.

Marks, J. (2009) *Why I Am Not a Scientist: Anthropology and Modern Knowledge*. Berkeley: University of California Press.

Marshall, E. (1998) The power of the front page of the *New York Times*. *Science*, 280: 996–997.

Mazumdar, P. (1992) *Eugenics, Human Genetics and Human Failings: The Eugenics Society, Its Sources and Its Critics in Britain*. New York: Routledge.

McAnany, P. A. and Yoffee, N., eds. (2009) *Questioning Collapse: Human Resilience, Ecological Vulnerability, and the Aftermath of Empire*. New York: Cambridge University Press.

Mekel-Bobrov, N., Gilbert, S., Evans, P., Vallender, E., Anderson, J., Hudson, R., Tishkoff, S., and Lahn, B. (2005) Ongoing adaptive evolution of ASPM, a brain size determinant in Homo sapiens. *Science*, 309: 1720–1722.

Nash, C. (2008) *Of Irish Descent: Origin Stories, Genealogy, and the Politics of Belonging*. Syracuse: Syracuse University Press.

Nelson, A. (2016) *The Social Life of DNA*. Boston: Beacon Press.

Pearson, K. (1892) *The Grammar of Science*. London: Adam and Charles Black.

Pollock, A. (2012) *Medicating Race: Heart Disease and Durable Preoccupations with Difference*. Durham: Duke University Press.

Peregrine, P., Ember, C., and Ember, M. (2003) Cross-cultural evaluation of predicted associations between race and behavior. *Evolution and Human Behavior*, 24: 357–364.

Proctor, R. and Schiebinger, L. L., eds. (2008) *Agnotology: The Making and Unmaking of Ignorance*. Stanford: Stanford University Press.

Rapp, R., Heath, D., and Taussig, K. (2001) Genealogical disease: where hereditary abnormality, biomedical explanation, and family responsibility meet. In *Relative Values: Reconfiguring Kinship Studies*, ed. S. Franklin and S. McKinnon. Durham: Duke University Press.

References

Reardon, J. (2004) *Race to the Finish: Identity and Governance in an Age of Genomics*. Princeton: Princeton University Press.

Regalado, A. (2006) Scientist's study of brain genes sparks a backlash. *Wall Street Journal*, June 16: A12.

Richardson, S. S. (2011) Race and IQ in the postgenomic age: The microcephaly case. *BioSocieties*, 6: 420–446.

Ripley, W. Z. (1899) *The Races of Europe*. New York: D. Appleton.

Rohde, D. L. T., Olson, S., and Chang, J. T. (2004) Modelling the recent common ancestry of all living humans. *Nature*, 431: 562–566.

Segal, N. L. (2012) *Born Together – Reared Apart: The Landmark Minnesota Twin Study*. Cambridge: Harvard University Press.

Seligman, C. (1930) *Races of Africa*. New York: Henry Holt.

Sergi, G. (1893) My new principles of the classification of the human race. *Science*, 22: 290.

Simpson, G. G. (1945) The principles of classification and a classification of mammals. *Bulletin of the American Museum of Natural History*, 85: 1–349.

Sinnott, E. W. and Dunn, L. C. (1925) *Principles of Genetics*. New York: McGraw-Hill.

Sollas, W. J. (1911) *Ancient Hunters: And Their Modern Representatives*. London: Macmillan.

Spiro, J. (2009) *Defending the Master Race: Conservation, Eugenics, and the Legacy of Madison Grant*. Burlington: University Press of Vermont.

Sussman, R. W. (2014) *The Myth of Race: The Troubling Persistence of an Unscientific Idea*. Cambridge: Harvard University Press.

TallBear, K. (2013) *Native American DNA: Tribal Belonging and the False Promise of Genetic Science*. St. Paul: University of Minnesota Press.

Tattersall, I. and DeSalle, R. (2011) *Race? Debunking a Scientific Myth*. College Station: Texas A&M University Press.

References

Teslow, T. (2014) *Constructing Race: The Science of Bodies and Cultures in American Anthropology*. Cambridge: Cambridge University Press.

Thieme, F. P. (1952) The population as a unit of study. *American Anthropologist*, 54: 504–509.

Thomas, M. G. (2013) To claim someone has "Viking ancestors" is no better than astrology. *Guardian*, February 25.

Tucker, W. H. (2002) *The Funding of Scientific Racism: Wickliffe Draper and the Pioneer Fund*. Urbana: University of Illinois Press.

Tutton, R., Smart, A., Ashcroft, R., Martin, P., and Ellison, G. T. (2010) From self-identity to genotype: the past, present, and future of ethnic categories in postgenomic science. In *What's the Use of Race*, ed. I. Whitmarsh and D. S. Jones. Cambridge: MIT Press.

Tylor, E. B. (1871) *Primitive Culture*. London: John Murray.

Wade, N. (2014) *A Troublesome Inheritance*. New York: Penguin.

Wade, P. (2002) *Race, Nature and Culture: An Anthropological Perspective*. London: Pluto Press.

Wade, P. (2004) Human nature and race. *Anthropological Theory*, 4: 157–172.

Wailoo, K. and Pemberton, S. (2006) *The Troubled Dream of Genetic Medicine: Ethnicity and Innovation in Tay-Sachs, Cystic Fibrosis, and Sickle Cell Disease*. Baltimore: Johns Hopkins University Press.

Washington, H. A. (2006) *Medical Apartheid: The Dark History of Medical Experimentation on Black Americans from Colonial Times to the Present*. New York: Doubleday Books.

Weiner, J. S. (1957) Physical anthropology – an appraisal. *American Scientist*, 45: 75–79.

Wilson, E. O. (1994) *Naturalist*. New York: Island Press.

Wolf, E. (1982) *Europe and the People Without History*. Berkeley: University of California Press.

Woods, F. A. (1918) Review of *The Passing of the Great Race*, 2nd edn. *Science*, 48: 419–420.

References

Wright, L. (1997) *Twins: And What They Tell Us About Who We Are*. New York: Wiley.

Young, M. (1928) The problem of the racial significance of the blood groups. *Man*, 28: 153–159, 171–176.

Yudell, M. (2014) *Race Unmasked: Biology and Race in the 20th Century*. New York: Columbia University Press.

Zimmerman, A. (1999) Anti-Semitism as skill: Rudolf Virchow's Schulstatistik and the racial composition of Germany. *Central European History*, 32: 409–429.

Index

Index

Index